DECISIVE WARFARE

OTHER BOOKS
BY REGINALD BRETNOR

GILPIN'S SPACE
THE ULTIMATE FEGHOOT

DECISIVE WARFARE

A Study in Military Theory

REGINALD BRETNOR

WILDSIDE PRESS
BERKELEY HEIGHTS • NEW JERSEY

DECISIVE WARFARE: A STUDY IN MILITARY THEORY

Published by:

Wildside Press
P.O. Box 45
Gillette, NJ 07933-0045
www.wildsidepress.com

FIRST WILDSIDE PRESS EDITION:
FEBRUARY 2001

To
my wife Helen
(1912-1967)

Acknowledgments:

To David Higham Associates, Ltd. and Rutgers University Press for permission to quote from Major-General J. F. C. Fuller's *The Conduct of War*.

To Constable Publishers, London, for permission to quote at length from F. W. Lanchester's *Aircraft In Warfare*.

To Princeton University Press for permission to quote from Herman Kahn's *On Thermonuclear Warfare*.

To Barnes & Noble, Inc. and George Allen & Unwin Ltd. for permission to quote from Michael Prawdin's *The Mongol Empire*.

To Colonel T. N. Dupuy, Executive Director of HERO, and to the editors of *Ordnance* for permission to reproduce tables from his article, "Tactical Nuclear Combat."

Contents

The vulnerability of man and his works to destructive force is an inescapable factor in every military equation, and no accurate evaluation or prediction of the processes of war is possible unless it is taken into consideration. Unfortunately, existing sets of "principles of war" do this only by implication. It is essential, therefore—especially at a time of unprecedented technological development—to understand the vulnerability factor and always to give it its proper weight in our military estimates.

The means and methods of expressing destructive force have changed radically over the centuries. The military principles governing its expression have not changed—nor have they ever been set forth in such a way that they may be applied universally. Descriptive terminologies accurate in one age often have been allowed to persist into another, when they apply no longer, and loose rules of practice have been mistaken for underlying principle. We must arrive at a general theory of the functioning of destructive force in the equations of war which will not fail us, regardless of changing values and situations.

Time is the third inescapable factor in the equations of war. Throughout the several phases—preparatory, logistics, maneuver, weapons—involved in the expression of destructive force, time is an absolute determinant both of force and of realized vulnerability, sometimes as a multiplier, sometimes as a divisor. Nothing has caused the loss of so many battles, campaigns, and wars as the failure to evaluate the time factor properly. Nothing has contributed so often to decisive victory as the ability to judge it accurately.

Chapter 4 The Critical Imbalance

The equations of war always have two sets of values: one's own and the enemy's. When these are too nearly balanced, the attrition of force tends to be slow, and action indecisive. When, by military art or natural circumstance, they are thrown sharply out of balance, attrition can be swift and action decisive. The battles and campaigns where decisive victories are achieved are usually those in which a critical imbalance has been established—that point of no return where, inevitably, the enemy's realized vulnerability escalates and his force decays. Therefore the critical imbalance should be the goal of all military theory, of all military planning, of all commanders.

Chapter 5 The Optimum Response

The ideal of the critical imbalance must never be forgotten, and no second-best solution should ever be accepted until, and unless, events inexorably force such a course. In many situations, naturally, no critical imbalance can be achieved, but if we always aim for it, then we will at least achieve an optimum response in terms of the military equations confronting us, and their values of destructive force, of vulnerability, and of time. We will then do the best we can, not just where courage and determination are concerned, but against the situational realities that dictate possibilities and limitations.

Index

PREFATORY COMMENT
1986

Seventeen years have passed since *Decisive Warfare* was published, twenty since I seriously began to write it, and about forty-five since the idea of doing so first occurred to me. My interest in the theory of war goes back to the years before World War II, when I read everything I could find on the subject. All the maxims and "principles of war" I came across seemed to me to lack the essential element of universal applicability and to provide no consistent basis for accurate prediction.

What do you do when a system of theory fails to satisfy you? Obviously, you either dismiss it from your mind, or, if your intellectual curiousity demands it, try to formulate a better one of your own. This I hesitated to attempt, because naturally I was inhibited by my lack of properly impressive qualifications. However I was fortunate enough to receive much encouragement from the late Colonel William Fergus Kernan, artillery officer and author, and to receive it at a time of great personal distress. Eventually I realized that had there existed any patterns of training or experience that would qualify one for such a task, then more satisfactory maps of cause and effect in war—which is all any system of military theory is—would long since have been set forth.

I did not begin to write the book until I arrived at the conclusion that any adequate analysis would have to be based on a *complete* separation of the purely physical processes of war and those less concrete and less easily measurable ones which direct and impel them: those of the human mind and will. This was the basis for the theoretical system elaborated in the book, and it will also provide the framework for my discussion of the changes which have taken place since the book's publication.

Decisive Warfare never became quite the book I wanted it to be. My original title for it was *The Processes of War*, which is what it is all about, but Stackpole, the publishers, did not like it. We also had disagreements on content and approach: for example, I was asked to delete all direct discussion of Vietnam— and this despite the fact that I was in no sense being a dove. And we had other differences. At any rate, when the book came out, it brought me both the best and worst reviews I had ever received: the best in *Ordnance*, where Brigadier General Ghormley, then editor, made it his *Book of the Month*; the worst a very brief sneer in the *Library Journal*, where from a sales standpoint it could do me most harm. Now, in considering this new edition, I have decided to let the text stand unaltered, and to devote this preface to discussing today's politico-military picture.

SCIENCE, TECHNOLOGY, AND
THE SEMANTICS OF WAR

It is axiomatic that, in any field, science and its resultant technologies progress—given adequate support—along steeply escalating curves. Their advance is geometrical, not arithmetical. Therefore, to cope with the enormous changes this implies, our own thinking must progress similarly.

Most decidedly, it has *not*. Too many of our statesmen and military leaders, even more of our media men, and, surprisingly, a great many of our scientists, still think in strictly linear terms. This is how our languages are structured—they have developed over the millennia to describe a world which either seems virtually unchanging or else changes very slowly. (This is also the reason why the physical sciences have been forced to invent their own, more realistic languages for the description and solution of specific physical problems.) The language of war has been no exception.

No events in the history of the world have

demonstrated the exponential nature of scientific progress more dramatically than atomic fission and hydrogen fusion, and no events have demonstrated more tragically the failure of our thinking processes to keep pace with that progress.

In Lord Tennyson's prophetic poem, "Locksley Hall," we find the following lines:

Yet I doubt not thro' the ages one increasing
    purpose runs,
And the thoughts of man are widen'd with the
    process of the suns.

If Tennyson's prophetic intuition was indeed referring to the process that keeps the stars' atomic furnaces alight (rather than to the pulse of our own sun's rising and setting), he seems to have missed the boat where the thoughts of his fellow men are concerned. I remember thinking, when I learned of what had happened at Hiroshima, that now, at long last, there would *have* to be a complete revolution in our attitudes toward war and peace. Instead, almost all of us, the man in the street and his leaders and whoever else did his thinking for him, continued to regard "the bomb" as though it really wasn't that much different from its chemical predecessors. Were our thoughts widened? Not so you could notice it.

This, in my opinion, was the most shocking lesson of the post-Hiroshima years, and even more shocking is the fact that there has been no real improvement since 1969. And this applies not only to nuclear weaponry, but also to the entire spectrum of weapons and their enabling devices: chemical and bacteriological weapons, radiation weapons of various sorts (lasers, particle-beam weapons, etc.), electronic "weapons" and the electronic elements of weapons systems, and whatever else awaits us. We simply have failed to achieve any full understanding of what is going on, and the innumerable limited wars which have taken place in the last two decades have taught us few valuable lessons, largely because their limitations have been imposed artificially.

MILITARY MYOPIA AND THE EQUATIONS OF WAR

In *Decisive Warfare*, I have set forth my own view of the physical processes of war in terms of unquantified equations, using terms which avoid certain of the inescapable connotations of older terminologies: M and M' for values of destructive force, one's own and the enemy's, V and V' for vulnerability values, T and T' for time; and in this discussion I shall refer to them without further elaboration. Let us consider the several areas in which our apparent picture of the physical processes of war fails to correspond with reality.

Our evaluation of V and V'. Perhaps because most sets of "principles of war" emphasize only positive factors, or perhaps because it is painful to admit to the fact of vulnerability, our tendency has been either to undervalue or virtually ignore it. A case in point is the fact that today we in the United States have virtually no civil defense system comparable, say, to those of Sweden or Switzerland. Our announced program for the evacuation of cities in event of a nuclear emergency is a tragic absurdity, as anyone but a bureaucrat would recognize. When a single bad freeway accident can snarl traffic for hours, when it can take half an afternoon to clear out a giant stadium, how can anyone in his right mind seriously consider the crash movement of hundreds of thousands of untrained, unprepared people?

Again, the response to greater M—let's say to firepower in the field—has inevitably been dispersal and taking cover, and the incredible firepower of nuclear weapons threatening our cities should have evoked a similar response. It has not. Ever since Hiroshima, we have been centralizing. A greater and greater percentage of our population and industries has been crowding into such areas as the highly vulnerable Southern California population complex. It may make economic sense, but it makes no military sense at all.

This brings us to another example: the increasing use of giant tankers and huge container ships. Here we find a single enormous vessel, now usually largely automated, doing the work of ten or twenty smaller ships, and with a minimal crew. Why? Because they are much more profitable for their owners. Do we ever ask ourselves of what value such concentrations of vulnerability will be as naval auxiliaries? Or where, in event of an emergency, we'll find trained merchant marine officers to man a suddenly expanded fleet? Or even whether we'll be able to rely on those operating under foreign flags of convenience?

From these floating monsters it is a natural step to their naval cousins: giant carriers and battleships. When *Decisive Warfare* was written, it was generally assumed that battleships were a thing of the past, and there were also excellent arguments against the retention of giant carriers. Yet now we are resurrecting the former and building even more of the latter, despite the lessons of Eniwetok and Bikini, of *Yamato* and *Musashi*, of *Repulse* and *Prince of Wales*. It seems as though their proponents are taking it for granted that there will be no use of nuclear warheads in any future major war; and yet it would seem obvious that the only area where these might conceivably be used without sparking a general nuclear conflict would be at sea, for certainly the sinking of a battlewagon or giant carrier would be less traumatic to a government or a populace than the use of nuclear weapons on land.

Good sense would seem to dictate that, as our weaponry becomes more and more powerful, we should seek to minimize our vulnerability at sea by mounting the most effective weapons possible on the cheapest, simplest, fastest platforms.

These points are discussed in *Decisive Warfare*, and if they were obvious almost twenty years ago, how much more obvious should they be today? However, it is not only V that we have failed to assess properly. We have also failed to appreciate fully the escalation of M, of destructive force.

While there appears to have been no significant

increase in the power of individual fission and fusion weapons, there has certainly been a very marked increase in their numbers and variety, and also—and this could conceivably be most important— almost certainly in their availability. There still are five hydrogen powers that we know of, and several conventional atomic powers of which we can be reasonably sure. But there has also been evidence that totally irresponsible nations—those who have consistently supported international terrorism—have been trying to attain atomic status. There is no basic reason why they cannot. In other words, what once was a simple Two-Power problem is now becoming an Nth-Power problem, with possible international complications that boggle the mind. Here we have the geometrical progression again.

Nor is this confined to atomic weaponry. Twenty years ago, lasers and particle-beam weapons, smart counter-weapon weapons, and radiation weapons expressly designed to act against the electronic complexity upon which we have now become so dependent, weren't much more than a gleam in the eyes of their developers and of science fiction writers. For that matter, our electronic revolution was then only newly hatched. All the evidence appears to indicate that these advances simply have not been adequately digested and understood. Our weapons and their enabling devices have become vastly more complicated, a complexity again proceeding according to a geometrical progression, and this has not made the business of war easier to understand or to conduct. Specialization, whether of weapons or anything else, inevitably breeds complexity, and we now have reached the stage where we can paraphrase Ben Franklin's

> For want of a nail, the shoe was lost;
> for want of a shoe, the horse was lost;
> for want of a horse. . .

by starting out with *for want of a byte*...

These increases in specialization and complexity have other unhappy consequences. Inevitably, the instrumentalities necessary to the proper functioning of these new weapons and devices themselves become more highly specialized and complex. Personnel training and procurement become more of a problem. And finally, there must be at least some dimunition of the *totality* of destructive force available.

Our forces today, on land and sea, in the air, and even in space, no longer have anything approaching the beautiful simplicity of, say, the Mongol armies, where every man was an expert mounted archer and swordsman, every man was equally mobile, no man needed a more involved supply system than his fellows, and every man could carry out every military function (with the single exception of the simple specializations required for siege warfare).

In our eagerness to develop new and superior specialized weapons and enabling devices, we seem to have forgotten the possibilities which may still exist in new general purpose weapons less dependent on complexities of supply and coordination. To my mind, the most promising area for exploration would seem to be that of lasers and other beam weapons. A scientific and technological quantum jump similar to that which gave us microelectronics, but in the area of power supplies, could provide us with some very flexible weapons indeed. Research in this area could be considerably more rewarding than money spent on highly vulnerable, obsolete floating fortresses. It is not completely inconceivable, too, that it might eventually help to liberate us from our dependence on fossil fuels.

THE EQUATIONS OF WAR
AND THE WAYS WE THINK

The equations of war are absolute and uncompromising. Their values change and change drastically with every advance of science and the technologies, but they themselves do not. Wishful thinking can make no difference to them. We can no more wish the Soviet threat away than Chamberlain could wish away the threat of Hitler. They simply will not accomodate themselves to our desires. On the contrary, it is we who must change our ways of thinking to make certain that they do not operate against us.

Let us take one example. I mentioned the increase in the size of merchant vessels and the corresponding decrease in their numbers and in the size of their crews. This is very much in the interest of their owners, but militarily it most emphatically is not in the interest of the United States. Again, the centralization of certain key industries undoubtedly makes a great deal of economic sense to their managers and stockholders, but does that justify the concentrations of vulnerability which inevitably ensue? If we wish not only to survive, but to prevail, in the world that is now taking shape around us, we must change this habit of thinking, both privately and on the governmental level.

Another area in which we have, in my opinion, drifted dangerously away, not only from the immediate practicality demanded by the realities of war, but also from our own military traditions, is in our new main reliance on a relatively small "professional" army. Today, we as a people are certainly not as close to our own armed forces as we were in the earlier years of the Republic, and because we are not—and because it is only too evident that, in any worst-case situation, the draft will be useless—a much lower proportion of the population has military skills and the discipline which their acquisition carries with them. We would do well to adopt some modification of the Swiss system of universal service, not as a substitute for the regular establishment, but as an active auxiliary to it. (Our present federalized National Guard does not fulfill this function, for service in it is much, much less than universal.) The argument that modern warfare is too highly technological for "part-time soldiers" doesn't hold water. It has been disproven in Switzerland and in Israel, though in each instance the "part-time" has been very considerably increased when necessary. The strange thing is that the mass media always seem ready to buy this argument, apparently not realizing the preponderance of part-time soldiers in our recent wars, if not in the highest command echelons, at least in all others. Men who are brought into the regular services in time of emergency do not, by virtue of their designations, become instant long-service veterans.

One area in which wishful thinking has long since triumphed over military good sense is that of international pacts and agreements. They have merit only where traditionally firm alliances are concerned: the United States and Great Britain, for example. Otherwise, their history is one of mendacity, or, more often than not, outright betrayal. Every arms limitation pact, every neutrality pact, every treaty of friendship and abiding peace, has proved meaningless when balanced against cold self-interest and unrestrained ambition. And yet we still go through the mumbo-jumbo of negotiating with governments who are our openly declared enemies, such as that of the Soviet Union, which has never renounced the *Comintern*'s declaration of war against capitalism and the free world. This has led us to such tragic absurdities as our reliance first on "mutual deterrence," then on "Mutually Assured Destruction" (M.A.D.). How many once-sovereign nations has the U.S.S.R. gobbled up since we first fell for these formulas in defiance of all the realities of war? How many have been swallowed just since *Decisive Warfare* was published?
This brings us to the vexing question of "arms control," of pacts like SALT I and SALT II, of the argument presently ensuing over General Daniel Graham's Strategic Defense Initiative (which the media have so ingeniously named "Star Wars",), and of the entire highly critical subject of the weaponry of the future.
It is a far cry from the semi-smart anti-tank projectiles, of, say, the 1967 Arab-Israeli War to the sort of *very* smart anti-rocket and anti-satel-

lite projectiles we currently have in our arsenals; or from the first primitive computers of the microelectronic revolution to the sort of communications processing and control equipment now operating combat aircraft, hovercraft, command centers afloat and ashore—or even field kitchens. Many long years ago, one might reasonably have expected to learn from any given war lessons valuable to the conduct of the next one. Today, this is only partially—and dangerously—true, for the odds are that the weapons and techniques of the previous war may very well be perilously obsolete by the time the next dust-up occurs.

Therefore, we can safely say that the only inevitably valid lessons we can learn from the small wars of the past few years are those which either illustrate the equations of war in principle, or those which give us some foretaste of the new technologies and what they might evolve into given what we know about the geometrical progression of science and technology. And we should remember that today we live on the cutting edge of more than forty years of what amounts to wartime secrecy, that secrets *can* be kept, and that it is highly unlikely that any power holding a weapon or device capable of a decisive technological surprise is going to use it in a local conflict not critical to its own survival.

This brings us to SDI and to the present debate over it. I personally am for it, though I do not believe that any anti-missile satellite defense can make us completely safe against attack. Modern war is too complex, and its instruments are developing too rapidly for that. Nonetheless, it certainly can lessen the Russian missile threat very effectively— which is probably why the Russians are so against it.

Why so many of our own scientists and media men are against it is harder to understand, especially when it is misrepresented. For example, a recent *Los Angeles Times* report quotes a story by R&D Associates, "an influential defense think tank," stating that,

...in a matter of hours, a laser defense system powerful enough to cope with the ballistic missile threat can also destroy the enemy's major cities by fire. The attack would proceed city by city, the attack time for each city being only a matter of minutes....After spending hundreds of millions of dollars, we would be back where we started from: deterrence by retaliation.

These conclusions are, in my opinion, gross oversimplifications, arrived at without due regard to those equations of war which govern such situations, and without even referring to present SDI planning. We can cite another news story, from the January 25th issue of the *San Francisco Chronicle*:

The government has awarded Lockheed Missiles & Space Co. in Sunnyvale a $468 million Star Wars contract to develop an interceptor that can smash enemy missiles 100 miles up in space...
Lockheed will build a non-nuclear, lightweight, low-cost interceptor that can destroy ballistic missile warheads by smashing into them above the atmosphere. The impact would harmlessly disintegrate nuclear warheads...
The...program is related to the homing overlay experiment, also conducted by Lockheed. On June 10, 1984 a Lockheed interceptor hit and destroyed a dummy warhead hundreds of miles up in space.

This scarcely sounds as though SDI's central thrust, at least at present, is toward a main reliance on lasers. However, if eventually it does develop in this direction, considering the comparative vulnerability factors of the United States and the U.S.S.R., I personally think it would be greatly to our advantage.
At its best, SDI will give us an effective defense against nuclear missile attack, and at its worst—it will at least restore something of the Two-Power balance; for the cost of lofting laser satel-

lites in adequate numbers and defending them in space will be beyond what nations which are less than super-powers will be able to afford, at least for some time.

SDI, despite the publicity it has received, may very well not be the only new weapons system in the offing, and in all our estimates of the situation we should never forget to take into consideration every area of scientific research and technological development. And we should never ignore the possibilities secrecy may conceal. Certainly we should never try to save money on basic research, for that is where quantum jumps originate, and it is these quantum jumps which, in a future major war, could conceivably be decisive.

Let us sum up the major changes in the physical values of the equations of war since 1969:

1. An exponential increase in the sophistication and power of weapons and enabling devices.

2. An exponential increase in the sophistication and power of weapons available to second- and third-rate powers and to terrorists.

3. A similar increase—and this we must not underrate—in the communications facilities available to fanatical and irresponsible leaders.

4. An actual increase in our areas and concentrations of vulnerability.

THE NON-PHYSICAL FACTORS AND THE EQUATIONS OF WAR

In *Foundations of the Science of War*, a brilliant and penetrating analysis which I have cited several times in this book, Major General J. F. C. Fuller wrote,

Mental force does not win a war; moral force does not win a war; physical force does not win a war; but what *does* win a war is the highest combination of these three forces acting as one force. Do not let us, therefore, belittle physical force, for it is an essential of this trinity, an all other forces are as nothing without it.

I myself consider the idea of the three forces acting as one force to be a misconception, obscuring the true role of military intelligence and military morale, whose importance lies in the part they play in the realization of M and in preventing an enemy realization of V. (This is discussed at some length in *Decisive Warfare*.) In any case, the converse of Fuller's statement is equally true: that physical force itself can be as nothing unless the intelligence and the will to ensure its realization are there.

In this regard, the past twenty years give us ample reason to look at ourselves critically:

Though we have apparently been able to prevent communist takeovers in a few Third World countries, there are many more where we have not, starting with Vietnam, and in some cases— notably Iran—our bumbling has lost us, not only an erstwhile ally—but hundreds of millions worth of American military equipment, some of it decidedly sensitive.

At home, the symptoms of social disintegration which started to become obvious during the Fifties and Sixties are now more flagrant than ever. From a military standpoint, probably the most dangerous aspects of this are drugs—and especially their increasingly wide public acceptance—then the rise in crime, and thirdly the increase in a variety of venereal diseases. In short, to a very great extent we have allowed what used to be a counter culture to become *the* culture, particularly of the immature. (As I write this, I have before me a news story regarding the arrest, on cocaine peddling charges, of John A. Zaccaro, Jr., VP candidate Geraldine Ferraro's son. Apparently the entire student body at his exclusive Middlebury College knew about his alleged activities—so much so that they were joked about in the college's annual newspaper satire issue! And the faculty? Who knows.)

Any viable society—especially any militarily viable society—must have rules to live by, and I think at this point we would do well to ask ourselves very soberly how many of us still do. The usual retort to this observation, that the Iron Curtain (and many other) countries have similar problems, including pervasive alchoholism in the Soviet Union, may well be true, but let us never be simple-minded enough to count on it or to use the possibility as an excuse for ignoring our own weaknesses.

Above all, let us never commit the error of scorning theory and exalting a specious practicality—something we can never afford to do in this age of constantly accelerating, often terribly sudden, change. We would do better to remember what Sir James Turner wrote in *Pallas Armata: Military Essayes of the Ancient Grecian, Roman, and Modern Art of War*, (London, 1683) three hundred years ago:

...Though the Art of War be a Practical one, yet the Theory is so needful, that without it you may be Common Souldiers good enough, but not good Commanders; you are to know more than you daily see; for it is a sign of a very mean Officer, when he tells you he likes not such a thing, because he never saw it before.

—Reginald Bretnor
Medford, Oregon
April, 1986

Preface

To paraphrase John Donne, *no book is an island.*
No book can be considered as wholly new, wholly original,
wholly independent of those others which have preceded
it in its own field or of the cultural continuity that produced
them all—for no man has ever written a book wholly out of
the resources which were his at birth. It would be impossible to do so. He would have to manage, not only without
a spoken language, but without all those experiences of
humanity and the human environment which make him
what he is. This is not to disparage the creative faculty and
the creative urge in man; it is simply to place them both—
and books in general, and this book in particular—in a
proper perspective.

An intellectual debt can never really be repaid; it can
only be handed on to others. Often, when it is owed to the
long-vanished past, the ultimate debtor is not even aware
that it exists. However, when it is immediate, when one
knows to whom one owes it, it should be acknowledged,
not parenthetically somewhere in the text, but at the outset. Therefore, I shall, here, reverse the ordinary order in
prefaces and begin with such an acknowledgment.

Any informed reader of this book will, I am sure, recog-

9

nize that much of it rests on the work of Captain Sir Basil Liddell Hart and of the late Major-General J. F. C. Fuller. My introduction to their books, in the early 1930's, not only stimulated my interest in the theory of war, but also encouraged me to hope that eventually a body of theory would be developed accurate and complete enough to enable the reliable prediction of war's events regardless of its changing conditions. Among the titles which impressed me most, and most enduringly, were Fuller's *The Reformation of War* and *Foundations of the Science of War*, and Liddell Hart's *Great Captains Unveiled, The Ghost of Napoleon,* and *A Greater Than Napoleon: Scipio Africanus.* These not only instructed and informed me, but even while I read them, pricked me into thinking, and I began to wonder whether I might not myself make some contribution in the field. If now, finally, I have failed in this book to do so, the fault is mine alone, and is certainly not shared by these splendid mentors.

Sporadically, during the 'thirties, I read, argued, took notes and then mislaid them, and labored under the delusion that I was trying to formulate a "science of war." The only appreciable result, in retrospect, was that my evaluation of the relevance of weapons—mortars in jungle warfare, for example—became rather more accurate than it might otherwise have been. In 1941, the late Colonel William Fergus Kernan, author of *Defense Will Not Win The War,* and (later on) of *We Can Win This War,* very kindly gave me much encouragement and urged me to develop, write, and publish what I had in mind. I did not do so, partly because of other pressures in those years, but mainly, I think, because subconsciously I realized that I was by no means ready to—that I was abstracting inaccurately and over-complicating everything in an area of enquiry where accurate abstraction and simplification were essential.

After I started freelancing in 1947, and for many years

thereafter, my efforts were only occasional. When a new book or a new situation or a new development in weapons came to my attention, and if other concerns did not interfere, I would take a few notes and then put them by. For one thing, I labored under the misconception that it would be virtually impossible for an "unqualified" civilian to publish on the theory of war in the service journals; in fact, I'm afraid that I said so forcefully and often. Therefore it is with some embarrassment that I now tender my apologies to Colonel Donald J. Delaney, Editor in Chief of the *Military Review*, who accepted and published the first two chapters of this book in abbreviated form—and confess to him that crow is not only edible, but sometimes downright tasty!

Three or four years ago, however, I again began to do some serious and protracted thinking on the subject, and finally, in 1965, I completed the shorter version of my chapter, "Vulnerability and the Military Equation." This brings me back once more to Sir Basil Liddell Hart, for after the chapter had appeared in the *Military Review* for September 1966, it was brought to my attention that he had pointed out the importance of the vulnerability factor many years ago, especially in his *Thoughts on War*,[1] published in 1944, a work which it was my ill fortune to miss entirely, and in two or three others which I may or may not have seen. Because of the possibility that I may have profited from one or another of these, I will quote his statement concerning vulnerability from the *Thoughts*, a statement originally noted down in November 1933:

On the relation between strength and vulnerability
A fundamental condition underlying the problems of defense is that security cannot be estimated purely in figures

---

[1] Liddell Hart, *Captain Sir* Basil, *Thoughts on War*, London, Faber and Faber Ltd., p. 155. 1944.

of armed strength. The strength of a country in war is not such a simple sum. Any calculation of strength must take into account the resources of a country for war, as well as its forces. But even this sum, so difficult to work out, is too simple for truth. The measure of a nation's military strength depends on the measure of its vulnerability to attack no less than upon its forces and resources. This factor of "vulnerability" has yet to be adequately appreciated, although it has grown immensely in importance under modern conditions, especially under pressure of air-power. It affects all calculations of war, from the highest scale, of the comparative defense situation of countries, down to the effect with which particular weapons can be credited.

The vulnerability of the target counts for at least as much as the power of the weapon—and possibly counts for more.

Vulnerability itself is a compound of factors. The relative vulnerability of a nation is affected not only by its geographical, but by its industrial, political, and even sociological conditions. The very industry that augments its strength for war may at the same time produce a counterbalancing degree of vulnerability. And the centralization of industry may counteract the growth of industry from a military point of view. Wise statesmanship would give as much attention to diminishing and dispersing the target offered to an enemy's forces as to developing its own forces.

In this swiftly changing world, there are few writers on military theory and world affairs whose works retain their freshness and their pertinence after forty, thirty, or even twenty years. In this respect, Liddell Hart's are virtually unique. No one, today, can write thoughtfully on the theory of war without being in his debt. It gives me great pleasure, therefore, to acknowledge once more my own indebtedness to him.

It has not been my purpose in this book to elaborate anything as presumptuous and unlikely as a rigid "science of war." The word *science* is used much too loosely today. On the one hand, it is applied to the exact sciences, where events are uniformly measurable and uniformly predictable. On the other, we find it used to describe academic disciplines with little or no predictability, and even activities which not long ago were considered rather simple skills. What I have sought to do, then, is to examine the processes of war *as processes*, penetrating wherever possible through the confusion which inevitably accompanies changing techniques and instruments, changing terminologies and definitions, changing relationships and policies. I have tried to isolate what *really* happens from what, judged by obsolete frames of reference, may *appear* to happen. In short, I have tried to provide new and different frames of reference by which contemporary and future military processes may be evaluated more accurately, and thereby to increase the factor of predictability in all matters pertaining to the use of armed force. I sincerely hope that I have, at least to some degree, succeeded—for we live at a time in history where any failure to predict the probabilities of conflict accurately can result in tragedy, not only to the nation, but to the world.

I owe a debt of gratitude above all to my late wife, Helen Harding Bretnor, without whose love and help and encouragement over many years this book could never have appeared; to her parents, Evelyn and the late Sidney T. Harding; to my sister Margaret, who also did much to make it possible; to the late Andrew Malozemoff, who first showed me Liddell Hart and Fuller; to the works of the late Count Alfred Korzybski; to my friend L. Macleod, who has often been a kindly and patient listener, and who will, I trust, be (in the words of that other good Scottish soldier, Colonel Robert Munro) a *"Noble, worthy, courteous, and loving Reader;"* and finally to all those writers, in the field and out of it, by whom I have more or less been educated.

REGINALD BRETNOR
Berkeley, California

13

Vulnerability And The Equations Of War

We live in an age of warfare. In this century, we have seen two world wars and uncounted major and minor ones, a few of them decisive, some of them protracted wars of delayed decision, more of them indecisive. Before discussing them and the purpose of this study, however, it should be clear that the basic concern is not whether a war is *actually* decisive in its effects on the peace which follows it—too many wars have been won by soldiers only so that politicians could throw away the fruits of victory— but with the question of how operations are conducted, and whether the war is won promptly, conclusively, and with a minimum of wasted effort. Perhaps this definition is wider than the normal connotations of the word *decisive*. We

14

The vulnerability of man and his works to destructive force is an inescapable factor in every military equation, and no accurate evaluation or prediction of the processes of war is possible unless it is taken into consideration. Unfortunately, existing sets of "principles of war" do this only by implication. It is essential, therefore —especially at a time of unprecedented technological development—to understand the vulnerability factor and always to give it its proper weight in our military estimates.

shall, nonetheless, let it stand, applying *decisive* in this sense not only to wars, but to warfare—to all those subordinate operations of which wars are composed.

In order further to clarify precisely what is meant, let us examine *indecisive* warfare. What constitutes an indecisive war or campaign or battle? Where war is concerned, the word can be applied accurately to any conflict which, even if "successfully" concluded, either fails to give the victor the power to achieve his political aims, or else costs him as much or more than the achievement of those aims is worth. This rule we can also apply to all subordinate operations, though here the standard for evaluation is not the ultimate aim of the war, but rather the degree to which the subordinate operations fail to implement those major operations of which they are a part.

Perhaps a few examples may be helpful. World War I was indecisive, regardless of how much power it gave the victors, because of its immense cost in blood and treasure, disorder and disruption; and the bloody "campaigns" on the Western Front, which accomplished almost nothing positive militarily, were indecisive subordinate operations. The Second World War was a protracted war of long-delayed decision. The Korean War started out to be decisive with the Inchon Landings, but ended up as indecisive because of subsequent errors. The Vietnam War, at least to the time of this writing, has been as apparently indecisive as any war ever fought. The Israeli-Arab War of June 1967 was a classical example of decisive warfare. Who knows what the next war, great or small, may be?

Only too frequently, attempts to determine why one war is decisive and another not, why one commander can achieve decisive victories while another accomplishes little or nothing, become confused by jealousies and enmities, by slurs and recriminations. This surely is due very largely to the fact that no "theory of war" exists accurate enough to enable precise and unemotional communication and criticism where matters of military controversy arise. Even the terminologies of Clausewitz and Jomini, of Mahan and Douhet, are now to some extent obsolete; they carry residues of ancient meaning no longer accurately applicable. When they are given an overlay of jargon misapplied from the physical sciences and social studies, confusion becomes even worse confounded: witness the too-frequent treatment of such subjects as "strategy" and "tactics" by men like Herman Kahn,[1] who can be allowed to typify the scientist trying to compute his way through a newly-discov-

---

[1] Kahn, Herman, *On Thermonuclear War*, Princeton, N. J., Princeton University Press, 1961.

ered and bewildering world of human affairs. It is not the purpose of this book, then, to duplicate these methods. Its purpose is simple: to try to understand those elements which are common to all wars despite changing conditions and changing instruments, and to see whether any more or less universal rules or laws can be derived which will apply anywhere, at any time, and under any conditions. If we can improve our understanding of the hows and whys of warfare in general, we will have taken another step toward the formulation of a true science of war, a science capable—for good or ill—of predicting military events with increased accuracy. If we can derive techniques from the laws governing these hows and whys, then we will have a useful instrument for the application of this science—even though that application will probably, except in certain special circumstances, always remain less of a science than an art.

Any body of theory is, in its essence, a map of how and why. It is a symbolic representation of the realities of structure and process; and its validity depends on the degree of correspondence between the representation and these realities, between the map and the terrain. Its applicability is, of course, determined by the degree to which it describes its area accurately, by the degree to which it describes erroneously, and by the degree to which it fails to describe at all. Therefore any theory which pretends to generality in any area must first be generally descriptive, excluding nothing which has occurred or can occur in that area, and then must be so generally accurate in its description that any discrepancies will be negligible in practice.

Thus, the theory of falling bodies adequately describes the fall of bricks or birdshot, fireworks or feathers, in vacuum or in air, in water or in molten lead, down to the surface of the earth or, like Icarus, into the flaming sun. It can describe the fall of objects yet to be invented, under conditions which may not yet exist; and the events, when they occur, will generally sustain its accuracy.

This is only a single, elementary instance. The evolving theoretical framework of the physical sciences holds many others, more inclusive and more impressive still. Indeed, it is the obvious practical applicability of these sciences which has led men to attempt the formulation of similarly applicable theories in the far more complex area of human relations: theories seeking to describe the fundamental mechanisms of conflict and coöperation. As yet, these have achieved no comparable measure of success. The social scientist especially, as prophet and as guide, is often no more reliable than the gypsy fortuneteller or the professional politician; we can even say that more has been accomplished towards a generally applicable theory of war than towards any which might govern the processes of peace. Therefore, in trying to forward the development of the theory of war into a science, we perhaps find ourselves on firmer ground than those who work in less dreadful, less destructive fields.

Here, the initial basis for the argument will be those "principles of war" which have been enunciated during the present century, and which have already had such a profound effect on military history, notably in World War II. This is tantamount to saying that this study takes its departure from the theoretical work of the late Major-General J. F. C. Fuller. It constitutes at once an acknowledgment of indebtedness to him and to others who have worked in the same field and an apology for the critical evaluation necessary if anything fresh is to be accomplished. The fact that we have chosen simply to use these "principles," which state a theory of war in its most concise and general terms, means only that more extended elaborations are not considered pertinent to the present thesis.

**The
Principles
of War**

In his preface to *The Foundations of the Science of War*,[2] General Fuller tells of his initial inability to find any clear statement of the principles of war, of his search for them, and of his formulation of the following set in 1912:

> The principle of the Objective.
> The principle of Mass.
> The principle of the Offensive.
> The principle of Security.
> The principle of Surprise.
> The principle of Movement.

He then relates how, in the *Journal of the Royal United Service Institution* for February 1916, he published an article entitled "The Principles of War with Reference to the Campaigns of 1914-1915," and added two more principles to the list:

> The principle of Economy of Force.
> The principle of Coöperation.

In 1920, these principles very slightly modified were included in British *Field Service Regulations*. In 1923, they were reprinted in Fuller's *The Reformation of War*. Finally, in 1926, in *The Foundations of the Science of War*, the following developed list appeared:

> (i.)   The principle of direction.
> (ii.)   The principle of concentration.

---

[2] Fuller, *Major General*, J. F. C., *The Foundations of the Science of War*, London, Hutchinson & Co. Ltd., (1926).

(iii.)   The principle of distribution.
(iv.)   The principle of determination.
(v.)   The principle of surprise.
(vi.)   The principle of endurance.
(vii.)   The principle of mobility.
(viii.) The principle of offensive action.
(ix.)   The principle of security.

The set of principles presently taught at the United States Army Command and General Staff College, derived at least in part from Fuller, illustrates the influence his work has had:

1. The principle of the objective.
2. The principle of the offensive.
3. The principle of simplicity.
4. The principle of unity of command.
5. The principle of mass.
6. The principle of economy of force.
7. The principle of maneuver.
8. The principle of surprise.
9. The principle of security.

Fuller's influence, while not always immediately obvious, did much to change the military history of our times. It probably would not be too much to say that his thinking, together with that of Captain Sir Basil Liddell Hart, was in a great measure responsible for the vast superiority of tactics and techniques in the Hitler War over their World War I counterparts.

In what sense, then, are these sets of "principles of war" lacking? And how, by examining them, can we begin to develop a new framework of theory capable of producing similar, and perhaps even greater improvements today and tomorrow?

These questions can best be answered by considering what these principles are, and what they are not.

In the first place—and this is rather more than a mere quibble over words—they should not, strictly speaking, be called *principles of war*. Other than indirectly, by implication, they do not describe the processes and relationships of war. Though derived from, and related to, a comprehensive and profound theory of certain of these processes and relationships, they themselves do not convey that theory.

Secondly, therefore, *they neither express a whole theory, nor do they constitute a whole science, of war.*

Instead, they may be termed *principles for the conduct of a war*—rules which, properly comprehended and adhered to by a commander, should bring him a high percentage of successes.

Thirdly, while an excellent case could indeed be made out for their immutability and universality, these qualities are not at once obvious and indisputable. Cases are numerous where one or more "principles of war" have seemingly been "successfully violated;" and this itself invites the suggestion that the principles themselves may be altered by the changing conditions of war.

In the first instance, above, it is stated that these principles do not accurately describe the processes and relationships of war; and the reason for repeating and emphasizing this statement is that no laws or principles which do not accurately describe processes and relationships can be relied on to predict or control them. To control, we must predict; to predict, we must describe accurately; to describe accurately, we must omit no essential element of the processes concerned.

As a matter of fact, the principles we are considering do in effect omit two such essential elements, considering them by implication only. Fundamentally, they state how one combatant may employ the forces at *his* disposal, for every principle but one—that of security—is (again except by implication) unilateral and *positive*.[3] In short, they do not include the forces of the enemy *directly and explicitly* in their descriptive framework, and, emphasizing the positive aspects of war, they virtually exclude from consideration the central negative factor of vulnerability.

If we are to attain descriptive accuracy, neither of these can be so excluded, for the major and minor processes of war alike can be described accurately only with whole equations, and without these two factors no whole equations can be written. In order to evaluate their proper role, it becomes necessary to reexamine the processes of war in general, reducing them to their simplest common denominators, defining them functionally, and at least suggesting the mathematical patterns of relationship which constitute the equations of war.

The Processes of War

The minor processes of war are fairly easy to understand and to describe. A bullet's flight from powder to target, artillery problems for units large and small, most questions of logistics—all these (except sometimes in their relation to the major processes) are subject to direct mathematical evaluation, prediction and control. So, more or less, are simple tactical problems, especially for small units or for large units simply used.

But the major processes of war are something else again. Only too often, their apparent complexity, the vast diver-

---

[3] In an alternative set of terms (*ibid.*), which in General Fuller's opinion, "More accurately express the energies they control," we find *surprise* replaced by *demoralization of force*, and *offensive action* by *disorganization of force*, thus reducing the unilateral orientation of that special set.

sity of the factors involved, and the scarcity or total lack of certain data eliminate the possibility of any direct mathematical—perhaps it would be better to say *of any direct arithmetical*—approach.

How, then, can we speak of the equations of war? Of what conceivable value is an equation which cannot be precisely written?

The answer to that is simple. It is true that the major processes of war can be of fantastic complexity. They are resultants of the interaction of innumerable minor processes. But this complexity, and the further complication of unknown and sometimes unknowable data, while it may exclude the type of mathematical analysis which depends on precise measurement in each and every situation, definitely does not exclude a mathematical approach similar to that of the algebras of logic, where it is the general cause-and-effect relationship structure of a process that is of first importance rather than exact quantitative measurement.

In other words, even if the equation cannot, for one reason or another, be precisely written, the knowledge of its structure—of its descriptive accuracy in principle—will be of inestimable value to prediction and control.

There are two elements which are basic to all the processes of war: the positive factor of might, of destructive physical force—which I will call M— and the equally important negative factor of *vulnerability*, or V, which has never yet had adequate emphasis. M measures destructive force pure and simple. V measures the vulnerability of man, his works, and his instrumentalities to destruction, *primarily by physical force.* In their interaction, the two are all-important, but neither can be of significance without the other.

In any military equation, each of these elements must appear in two aspects, representing the positive and negative values of the contending sides, thus: M and M', V and V'; and therefore every military equation *must* contain at least these four fundamental expressions.

All the other factors of war, in whatever situation, can be nothing more than their determinants.

The Negative Factor

There is an excellent psychological explanation for the fact that writers on the theory of war have failed to derive and emphasize *vulnerability* as a factor equal in importance to the positive factor of destructive force. In battle, the soldier must of necessity more or less ignore his own vulnerability; the commander must more or less ignore that of his men. The result has been an almost universal tendency, where military theory is concerned, to think too bravely—as the often tragic slowness in developing techniques for the reduction of vulnerability will witness. The important thing is to understand that the admission of vulnerability as an intrinsic human attribute, and of the factor of vulnerability in war, is indicative neither of cowardice nor of sick caution. Here we encounter a borderline of practicality and sanity. We can admire the daring of a Commodore Harwood, fighting *Graf Spee* with his vulnerable light cruisers. Would we admire him, or would we consider him an utter fool, if he had attempted the same action with wooden ships and muzzle-loading guns? Similarly, we can regard with admiration the apparent heedlessness of vulnerability which made the successful assault on Iwo Jima possible, and which actually revealed that the commanders concerned had evaluated this factor accurately—but we need not approve of any flat denial of vulnerability, whether it be by the mad Khalifa at Khartoum, by some mutton-headed tactician of World War I, or by one of the sorry present-day journalists or politicians who argue against a few extra billions for military or "civil" defense.

Briefly, there can be no militarily valid case against the admission and accurate evaluation of vulnerability. It may be true that, beyond appropriately stipulated limits, lower echelons should not concern themselves unduly with the problem—but it remains a problem of which high command should always be conscious simply because it is a physical fact of war, and an absolute determinant in every military equation not only of value relationships, but of that which is possible and that which is not.

Granting this, we must analyze this V factor, beginning with the natural circumstance from which it derives, and continuing with certain of the operative factors which determine its value in any given military equation.

Intrinsic Vulnerability

The human body is vulnerable to physical force, and it is from this intrinsic vulnerability that all possible values of the V factor in war derive. Militarily, it is a vulnerability of function—of the capacity to express destructive force directly or indirectly—for it must be understood that this is the sole value of the human organism in the military equation. From it derives the vulnerability of man's instruments and agencies of war, for even the vulnerability of a machine to damage or destruction is important only as it finally influences the expression of destructive force by or against human beings. From it, too, derives man's vulnerability to destructive psychological forces, for these also would have no military weight had they no physical effect.

Intrinsic vulnerability, then, is the physical vulnerability of the human body to destructive force:

1. In the direct expression of that force.

2. In our absolute dependence on maintenance, and our vulnerability to the consequences of destructive force expressed against the sources, materials and mechanisms of this maintenance.

The fundamental unit of V in the military equation, then, is the intrinsic vulnerability of the individual human being, for if it did not exist wars as we know them could not occur. Its basic value does not alter, for neither training nor magic nor modern medicine can render a human being even slightly bullet-proof or bomb-proof (although body or other armor does to a degree where its use is practicable). The maximum value of V in any military equation can therefore be set at *1*, which indicates the complete vulnerability of a man to destructive force expressed against him. Any more favorable situation must be expressed in terms, say, of decimals of 1.

To simplify matters, we can say that if effective force is expressed against a man whose realized vulnerability is 1 he is a dead man, or at least a man out of action. It is not surprising, as a consequence, that a great part of the technique and the art of war has always consisted of attempts to reduce either the man's vulnerability to the direct expression of destructive force or else to reduce his situational vulnerability with regard to the quantity or quality of force expressed against him.

The Reduction of Vulnerability

We have seen that the fundamental value of intrinsic vulnerability *cannot* be reduced. However, its realized value can, and throughout history only two basic methods of accomplishing this have been developed.

The first is the *interposition*, between the man and the force expressed against him, of substances less vulnerable than he—the parrying blade of a sword, armor, earth, sandbags, stone walls, solid granite, reinforced concrete.

The second is through the *dispersion* of men and, later, of machines—the intrinsic units of vulnerability—over the area where destructive force may be expected to express itself, so as to diminish the realized vulnerability-to-area ratio.

Mobility and obscurity, which at first glance might also appear to reduce the value of the vulnerability constant, on closer examination are found to do nothing of the sort. Mobility reduces the time factor in the military equation, which can be a multiplier of realized vulnerability and a divisor of destructive force. Obscurity, in certain situations and where destructive force is limited, simply makes it difficult to express that force effectively. Essentially, it involves "interpositions for concealment" which do not necessarily reduce the physical vulnerability of the target—the dark of night, a smokescreen, mist or fog or clouds, a hedge, a wheatfield.

As available force increases, the two basic methods become obligatory. Armor is worn against swords and spears of bronze or steel. Chargers are barded. Castles rise. Against Gustavus' galloping artillery, masses of cavalry thin out. Against the rifle, three ranks give way to two, and two to one. Now men advance as skirmishers and fire their pieces belly to the ground. Against machine guns and rapid-fire artillery, trenches—then foxholes—become the order of the day. The rule is simple. Disperse. Take cover. Or die.

To this there is *no* alternative, and temporary expedients

—even those which appear most plausible—are no valid substitutes. As destructive force intensifies, as its several spheres of expression are extended, the realized value of individual and group vulnerability *must* be reduced proportionately. The proof of this is that it inevitably *is* so reduced, even if, too often, tragically too late. There can be *no* return to the tactics of a previous age, when the values of destructive force were lower.

The best evidence of this lies in the object lesson of those instances when the rule has been ignored. Omdurman is one example—and one of the clearest. So are the 1915 artillery battles on the Somme. So, in a sense, are the fire raids on Tokyo.

The effect of the rifle and machinegun, of quick-firing artillery, of trench mortar concentrations and of tanks, of assault and bombardment aviation, and ultimately of nuclear weaponry and guided missiles—that effect is permanent and irreversible. Military methodologies have inevitably been forced to conform to better weapons in the past, even though frequently that conformance has been long delayed and dearly purchased. They must, quite as inevitably, conform to them now and in the future. The values of available destructive force, over their various areas of expression, eventually become the absolute dictators of strategy and tactics—in war. In peace, they seldom are, because too few men can perceive the inevitable cause and effect relationships involved. The terrible incentive to see clearly is not there.

This is of crucial importance, especially now. New weapons of unprecedented power are being introduced—some of them openly enough, others under impenetrable security restrictions—but the intrinsic vulnerability of men remains a constant. To what extent, then, can we disperse? To what degree can we interpose armor, and field fortifications, and overhead earth or rock cover for vital installations? In how many instances will we be able to substitute relatively invulnerable mechanisms for vulnerable human flesh? My impression—and of course based only on fragmentary and publicly available information—is that the world has not thought these problems through; that we still are trying to adapt the new and powerful to the old and now inadequate, rather like those Nineteenth Century geniuses who mounted Gatling guns on camel saddles; that perhaps we are relying too much on computers for our answers, without considering the possible artificiality of some of the problems they are asked to solve.

A further complication, and one which involves much more than weapons evaluation and the prediction of techniques, has been the change in military decision-making. We have moved out of the Renaissance, through the Industrial Revolution, into the age of the Scientific Revolution, and in doing so we have left behind the Universal Man and have found the Specialist. It used to be that those men, civilian and military alike, who participated in the decision-making process on the higher levels were, by and large, widely-read men with excellent general educations, and frequently the civilians themselves were ardent amateurs of war: Theodore Roosevelt and Winston Churchill come instantly to mind. Today we find their place being taken by men of vast but very different competence, men who have acquired the survival skills of a greatly changed society, and whose education often seems to have been designed only for the acquisition and sharpening of these skills: physical scientists, social scientists, cost accountants, specialized administrators and executives from the separate worlds of business and of government. The problem here is not, of course, whether we should employ these specialists, for obviously we must and will, but rather how we can employ them to best advantage. Any specialist is, in a military sense, a specialized weapon, and like other specialized weapons he will have unusual powers and unusual vulnerabilities. The first, being positive, will be easier to understand. The second, being negative and less apparent, require closer consideration in order to make certain that they are not transferred to organizations and doctrines with which the specialist is involved.

Vulnerability
of the Body
Military

The vulnerability of the military organism in war derives from the intrinsic vulnerability of man and his works, but it is much more than the sum of the individual vulnerability values involved. One might, here, begin to speak of tactical vulnerability and strategic vulnerability, but the meaning of the terms "tactical" and "strategic" has become so muddled, and they are now used so carelessly both by civilian writers and by many of the military, that a different approach is preferable.

The several ways in which a military organization is vulnerable as an organism to the expression of destructive force are all analogous to the ways in which the parts and functions of the human body are vulnerable. The body military has its directing mind, its nervous and digestive and circulatory systems, its senses, its tendons and muscles. By their nature, at any given time, they dictate its functional vulnerabilities, which are those:

1. Of command.
2. Of co-ordination.
3. Of the power to move (actually an aspect of 4 and 5, below.)
4. Of maintenance.
5. Of the power to express destructive force.

The body military may, like an individual, be confused, rendered semiconscious, or driven into nervous breakdown. It may be paralyzed, starved, or maimed, or suffer the amputation of its members. As its parts and functions are interdependent in their positive aspects, so are they, in varying degrees, in their vulnerabilities.

Like the individual, too, the body military may be vulnerable either by reason of its structure or by reason of its situation. *Structural vulnerability* can be simply illustrated. The combinations of man, horse, and sword, and of man, horse, and lance are vulnerable in different ways when under attack by similar combinations: the swordsman from the left rear, the lancer from the right rear. Similarly, bodies of 18th Century infantry, because of their normal formations and weapon characteristics, were highly vulnerable to fire or assault from the rear and flanks. All military instruments and instrumentalities possess their own structural vulnerabilities, determined by the nature of their components, severally and in combination; and any doctrine governing their employment, or the employment of destructive force against them, must take these into account.

Situational vulnerability is a rather more complex matter. It is determined partly by the character of the elements involved, partly by the physical environment in which they operate, and partly by their relationship one to another. Again, it can be illustrated simply. Troops deployed along a true crest and silhouetted against a skyline are situationally vulnerable compared to others deployed along a military crest. So are cavalry forced to charge up hill, or forces which have outrun their supplies or reinforcements, or armies operating separately without adequate liaison. Situational V should naturally be avoided whenever possible, while situational V' (the vulnerability of the enemy) should always be sought and exploited.

Psychological vulnerability, like physical vulnerability, is something all men share—though in widely varying degrees. No area of warfare promises the astute commander richer rewards or holds more terrible pitfalls for the blunderer, for its evaluation can pose immensely subtle and complex problems. It must be understood, as a basic principle, that psychological vulnerability is *not* something completely separate from the functional vulnerabilities previously enumerated, and that it is indeed important *only* as it affects these vulnerabilities. There can be no psychological vulnerability *unless its realization produces a physical effect on the military equation.*

The next chapter discusses the phases of expression of destructive force in war. For the moment, it is enough to say that the several types of functional vulnerability themselves exist *only* in their relation to this expression; in every instance, the vulnerability of the body military must be judged by the effect its realization will have on the ultimate ability to express M and M'. If the effect promises to be negligible, then there can be no point in wasting energy on its realization; if the effect is certain to be drastic, then any reasonable expenditure of energy will be justified.

Concentrations of Vulnerability

The principle of mass (the concentration of force) has as its direct counterpart the principle of the concentration of vulnerability. Obviously, concentrations of vulnerability should be avoided whenever possible, whether they be literal concentrations of vulnerable targets or tactical/strategic focuses of the vulnerability of function.

Thus, in the first instance, the horse is itself a concentration of vulnerability—a large area of fragile flesh naked to the weapons of the enemy. A body of horsemen is a similar concentration, rather greater than the simple sum of its units. One might have been justified in thinking that the universal adoption of weapons capable of taking full advantage of this factor would have made the obsolescence of the cavalry immediately apparent, and the fact that it did nothing of the sort illustrates the much too frequent unreality of peacetime military thinking.

One of the most perfect examples is that of *"portée"* cavalry. This was a French notion of, I believe, the 1920's. It contemplated the mass transportation of cavalry in large trucks. A column of almost solid horsemeat—a regiment, let us say—was to go roaring off down the highway at a velocity of twenty or twenty-five miles per hour; then, reaching its destination all fresh and eager, it was to disembark, mount up, and start riding around. En route, of course, it would have been able to disperse at only a fraction of the speed of cavalry riding along in column of fours—and all this in the age of attack aviation, to say nothing of accurate artillery! Even in the United States, *portée* cavalry units persisted until after the outbreak of World War II, and ordinary cavalry received some training in this form of transportation. Happily, there appears to be no record of anyone ever having tried to employ it seriously in combat.

In the second instance, where a focus of functional vulnerability is concerned, it is unnecessary here to give many examples. However, the fall of France provides an outstanding one—the German rupture of French defenses, rendering impotent the immobile destructive force concentrated in the Maginot Line, and negating utterly the expensive reductions of vulnerability achieved by its fortifications.

By defining vulnerability as an ever-present factor in all military processes, and by evaluating it accurately, we may be able to avoid similar errors and similar tragedies in the future. While it is never pleasant to criticize military instruments to which a great many people are devoted, three are here suggested which could possibly turn out to be today's counterparts of the cavalry if any major war—even a more or less limited major war—were to start. The first of these is the giant *aircraft carrier*. It concentrates men, money, weapons—yet one nuclear warhead can send it to the bottom. Another, very much in the news today, is the *helicopter*. It has some of the disadvantages of the horse, with a few peculiarly its own: it is slow by today's aircraft standards, noisy, and highly vulnerable. While it is extremely useful against technologically inferior opponents in limited wars, it may only be a matter of time before simple specialized weapons are developed to counter it. It will undoubtedly continue to have its uses, but I doubt that these uses will long be immediately tactical. The third instrument with a dubious fighting future is the *manned aircraft* (i.e., not a missile). It will take much longer to be phased out than the giant carrier or the helicopter; indeed, if a major *conventional* war were to break out today the role of the tactical manned aircraft could be quite as important as that played by the Israeli airforce in 1967. However, for reasons discussed later, the handwriting on the wall seems clear even for manned suborbital quasi-missiles, at least as major weapons.

Time, Movement and Vulnerability

Time, in the military equation, is a multiplier both of vulnerability and of destructive force; therefore it has always been in the interest of armies and navies to be as mobile as possible. Often, of course, mobility has not seemed to be an imperative. Speed was scarcely considered in designing the line-of-battle ships of the 18th Century. Nor, except by contemporary comparative standards, can it really be said to have entered seriously into the picture of European infantry warfare in those days. But breech-loading cannon, rifles, and machine guns began to change the picture. Speed reduces the total value—the beginning-to-end value —of *realized* vulnerability. Speed, through the movement of weapons, increases the radius of expression and the effectively-expressed value of destructive force. But, as in measures of dispersion and interposition, so must there be some realistic balance between the speed of that which is vulnerable and the speed of the destructive force directed against it or over the area it must traverse.

Thus, cavalry has "mobility." In the days of Brown Bess, this mobility was adequate to prevent a great many casualties and so allowed free battlefield movement of cavalry. By the time of the Boer War, the Russo-Japanese War, and World War I, it began to be obvious that this was no longer the case. The static nature of the Western Front in the Kaiser War was permitted to obscure this; and wishful thinkers, blaming the impotence of cavalry on the trenches, delayed the logical denouement until World War II.

No one, nowadays, will deny that, were it possible to breed a hundred-mile-an-hour horse, its greater mobility would no more revive cavalry than it would revive Belisarius. Mobility means nothing if weapons are able to saturate an area in less time than it takes to traverse it—or, alternatively, if it is inadequate to prevent destructive force from focussing effectively.

Here we have an interesting situation. In times past, mobility could effectively minimize the realized value of vulnerability very largely because of the natural lag, mental and physical, between human action and inaction. The horseman is out of range before he can be fired on; the surprised gunners cannot bring their pieces to bear; even the column of infantry, coming under artillery fire, can disperse and take cover to diminish its casualties.

It is precisely here that the great change has taken, and is taking, place. Rapidly, in more and more of war's processes, the mental and physical reactions of men are being replaced by those of machines. The eye of the gunner is beginning to be replaced by the far less fallible eye of the machine. The body and mind of the pilot, limited in the number of g's they can take, limited in their speed of reaction, are being replaced by mechanical and electronic gadgets not so limited.

In this connection, let us return to the subject of manned aircraft: their past, present and future. It would seem a very strong case can be made for the contention that the idea of an independent Air Force, constituting a true separate service comparable to the Army and Navy, was originally an error. Functionally, the military aircraft has, in the most important of its roles, been simply a step in the artillery and guided missile cycle—a slow projectile doing well enough until faster, more potent and less vulnerable projectiles came along. Its prime objectives have been on land and sea, and its only air combat function has been the negative one of preventing the enemy's air force from impeding its efforts or from attacking the land and sea objectives of its own side; in other words, the only importance of its air combat function has been with reference to the ultimate effect on these land or sea objectives. It has performed, and still is performing, other functions, some of which traditionally were the province of the cavalry. But essentially it has always been an extension of military power ashore and naval power over water, tied by gravity and its short flight time to land and sea. "Airpower," in the Douhetian sense of the word, has never existed.

Despite all this, it now seems probable that the error of

forming a separate Air Force was a fortunate one, and that its independence will be legitimatized, not in its present role, but in its emergent transformation into a Space Force. Once we really escape earth's envelope of air, and create such a force free of daily dependence on earth bases—which we are approaching and eventually will do—we will find it to be as much at home in its own element as armies and navies have been in theirs.

Today, it is only necessary to consider the increasing variety and sophistication of unmanned projectiles and guidance systems, and to extrapolate the probable curves of their future development, to see that as time moves on even the most advanced tactical manned aircraft must lose more and more of their usefulness in war.

In an age when we can speak seriously of interceptor missiles seeking out and knocking down other missiles moving at upwards of 250 miles a *minute,* it is difficult to foresee a profitable military future for far more vulnerable structures traveling at a fraction of such speeds, and guided by fragile computing systems—ourselves—incapable of tolerating the strains and stresses of extreme speeds and multiple gravities.

We are dealing, today, with completely new *orders* of destructive force, with completely new *orders* of speed, of accuracy, of reaction time, and of mechanical *invulnerability.* We would do well to revaluate our own intrinsic vulnerability, as well as all the military measures we can employ to reduce its potential value to an enemy. For, to any reasonably sane statesman, war must always be, not a game of Russian (or should we now say Chinese?) roulette, but a means to survival.

Obscurity
and
Vulnerability

It has been pointed out that obscurity, in itself, does not

physically reduce the value of realized vulnerability. Thus, a man walking across a field in dead of night is physically quite as vulnerable to rifle bullets as if he were walking at high noon, but any rifleman without an infra-red device is much less likely to hit him.

Obviously, the military value of obscurity declines as the radius of expression and the intensity of destructive force go up. However, this decline is by no means as dramatically apparent when the obscurity derives—as it does frequently —from the physically effective interposition of less vulnerable substances. Thus, forested terrain—and especially jungle—usually provides both types of interposition over extensive areas. Projectiles with relatively flat trajectories "see" it, in their primary phase, as a solid wall of wood, and in their secondary phase, after fragmentation, as an interrupted wall.[4] The eye directing the weapon, on the other hand, sees it as a more or less solid mass of verdure, depending on the range, position, and density of local growth. The combination, as almost everyone who fights a jungle war learns eventually, can make for very difficult situations indeed; and these situations, frequently, cannot be economically resolved without a thorough revaluation of all the factors of the military equation, V and V' especially. Where obscurity, for example, allows the free movement of a technologically inferior enemy, advantage should be taken of one's own technological superiority to provide means to lessen that obscurity. Similarly, where heavy cover renders an enemy relatively invulnerable to weapons which would prove decisively superior in more open warfare, specialized weapons, capable of nullifying that cover or diminishing its effect, should be provided. It is both

---

[4] I was first impressed by this "projectile's view" of forested terrain when, many years ago, I read of a World War I German infantry company occupying trenches in a small woods into which thousands upon thousands of shells were dropped—and suffering only a handful of casualties.

foolish and wasteful to rely merely on increasing the number of weapons proven indecisive and of instrumentalities proven vulnerable.

Vulnerability
and the
Nation

The principles of war, and this includes the principle of vulnerability, apply equally to military organizations and to the nations which employ them. We are still suffering a hangover from more civilized times, when nations and their armed forces were separate in men's minds; and we still speak of war as though it were a natural force beyond man's control.

War is not a phenomenon apart from man, like a seismic wave, a hurricane, a flood. War is something that men *do,* and as long as men appear determined to do it, as long as men prepare to do it without restraint, the nation must be regarded as a military organism, fully involved in the equations governing future wars, and involved no differently than a missile submarine, an infantry division, a hardened ICBM site. This, very strangely, is a factor not yet fully comprehended. We still speak of "civil" defense, for instance, as though it were something as far removed from the serious business of waging war as it seemed to be in 1915, and we refuse to recognize the fact that the vulnerabilities of the national organism are as critical to survival as are those of the armed forces themselves.

In a democratic country, certainly, it is not the place of the military man to dictate policy, domestic or foreign. However, he must always take it into consideration when planning how to implement it if the necessity arises. Similarly, no book on the general theory of war can afford to ignore the policy of nations in matters military, for national policy and military policy are inescapably interdependent. Each must be based realistically on the capacities and limitations of the other. Therefore the following paragraphs are addressed not so much to military readers as to those civilians, whether they be voters only or holders of high office, who ultimately determine both.

The day the first atomic bomb was detonated, it should have been obvious to students of war that a completely new order of destructive force had been introduced into the equations of war, and that the other values of those equations would probably have to be adjusted accordingly. It should have been obvious that, failing any sensible attempt to impose an effective world order, the rule that says *"Disperse. Take cover. Or die."* would henceforth apply more terrifyingly, more inflexibly, than ever before, and that any great power determined to survive would therefore do well to minimize its concentrations of vulnerability as speedily as possible, by dispersing them when it could, by digging in when critical concentrations could not be dispersed.

Most nations have done precisely the reverse. No real effort has been made to decentralize great cities and the supply, water and power networks on which they depend from day to day. Here in the United States, partly because of the mechanization of agriculture, we have witnessed the migration of vast numbers of people—many of whom are technologically unemployable—to megalopolitan centers. Instead of planning and subsidizing a spreading out, we have brought a once-dispersed population into prime target areas. Instead of concentrating on research into the desalinization of sea water, we have built huge new dams and are planning to build more—each a new concentration of vulnerability. Instead of emphasizing the development of small atomic power plants and research into solar power, we have pushed hydroelectric installations and the development of even more complex and interdependent power networks—like those which, allegedly through cumulative overload, blacked out so large an area of the Northeastern United States a few years ago.

It is true that, at our present technological level, economic determinism works towards centralization. It is cheaper for manufacturers and distributors to be at or near the focal points of transportation, power, or labor supply—so much so that vital social and military considerations can easily be forgotten. Highly competitive industries can hardly do otherwise, but the role of Government in the process is another matter. A great decentralization, especially of new industry, could have been accomplished through the wise expenditure of public funds which have, in many instances, been far less usefully employed: through direct subsidy, adequate corporation and tax allowances, the preferential awarding of government contracts, and, perhaps above all, a defense-oriented allocation of moneys for relief.

We now have perhaps ten percent of our people on the land; Russia has somewhere around seventy percent; China's dispersed percentage is even higher. We should not need to be reminded that it is far, far harder to cut off the food supplies of a million families working wheat fields or rice paddies than to shut off the supply lines to a great city; that it is infinitely easier to destroy one reservoir than twenty thousand wells and springs and rivulets.

An extreme example of militarily perilous centralization is the entire artificial population and industrial complex centering on Los Angeles and now embracing most of Southern California. It is completely vulnerable, directly and logistically. An enemy would not even need nuclear devices to reduce it: a few blockbusters dropped or otherwise introduced behind half a dozen major dams would literally kill it as a functioning, producing entity. Northern California is not yet quite so badly off, but before long—unless the trend is reversed—it will be. We cannot count on defensive weapons to protect such concentrations; it is far better to eliminate our vulnerabilities than to rely on uncertain protective measures.

Nor can the world really rely, as it is relying, on the idea of *deterrence*. We should remember always that only *sane* men can be deterred, and that in our lifetimes most of us have seen more than one madman, and many more whose sanity was questionable, wielding unassailable and absolute power. Today, after the crazy proliferation of new sovereign nations which followed World War II, the chances of such men emerging are greater than they ever were—and the natural functioning of the scientific method ensures that some of them at least will secure superweapons. It is naive to think that great powers organized for maximum vulnerability will be as able to deter the use of such weapons as they would be if they were organized for minimum vulnerability instead.

There is an atmosphere of unreality about some of the most solemn discussions of this subject, in such authoritative publications as, for example, the *Bulletin of the Atomic Scientists:* the estimates of casualties in eight and even nine figures, the pros and cons of emergency evacuation, the arguments for fallout shelters, the discussions of the economic impracticality of any all-out civil defense, and the pervading feeling that none of the participants has grasped the fact that he is talking about what can happen to real people in a real world. To my mind, this sort of thing has for years been typified by a "Civil Defense message" I heard over a local radio station in the 1950's. In her most saccharine commercial voice, the woman announcer informed her audience that "experts" then considered it probable that the United States would take some seventy-five million casualties in the first twenty-four hours of a nuclear war—but that it would not be enough just to absorb these casualties; we would have to come up fighting.

Is it not a bit unworldly to expect of the slums and suburbs of Los Angeles, Chicago, New York or Detroit something which first-rate combat divisions—with all their discipline and all their supportive elements—cannot always manage? Unhappily, this sort of thing is not confined to female announcers. Physical scientists proclaim it *ad nauseum;* journalists echo it; and it is even found in the utterances of professional military men. People who have waited half an hour and more while a major university tries to evacuate its football stadium, people who have observed traffic on a freeway stalled for two hours because a truck and trailer rig collided, people who have seen New York brought to a grinding halt by a railroad strike or power failure, people who have watched rioting mobs run amok to destroy entire square miles of the cities where they live— these people still seemingly cannot visualize the degree of disruption a major nuclear attack would bring to a great and complex nation with only a token Civil Defense policy.

Oddly, too, these attitudes are invariably accompanied by the assumption that the rest of the world would obligingly sit back, forgetting any resentments and ambitions, and allow us to recoup our shattered strength without attempting to destroy us or even to seize a fraction of our territory.

We must learn to be more realistic. At times, out of military necessity, the physical fact of vulnerability has to be ignored. But there are also times when, for the same good reason, it *must not* be. The dividing line can be determined by an understanding of the equations of war and their functioning, and by a sane discrimination between the possible and the impossible.

Destructive Force And The Equations Of War

Every departure from an accepted terminology should be justified by the realities which that terminology attempts to describe, and it may well occur to the reader now to question why the apparently redundant term *destructive force* is employed instead of, say, "armed force" or "military force," both of which may seem entirely adequate and perhaps synonymous. The reason is simple. To be effective, military force must be capable of destroying. It must be capable of destroying *in its contemporary context of situation and technology.* When it loses that capacity, even though it may wear the uniform of force, it cannot be so considered in the equations of war. It becomes shadow, not substance.

44

This means and methods of expressing destructive force have changed radically over the centuries. The military principles governing its expression have not changed—nor have they ever been set forth in such a way that they may be applied universally. Descriptive terminologies accurate in one age often have been allowed to persist into another, when they apply no longer, and loose rules of practice have been mistaken for underlying principle. We must arrive at a general theory of the functioning of destuctive force in the equations of war which will not fail us, regardless of changing values and situations.

Destructive force, then, or M, is more than merely "military force." It is *relevant* military force, and its value cannot be assessed without first measuring this element of relevance in terms of the basic factors of the military equation. It is by no means enough to evaluate the intrinsic destructive capability of weapons, of units, of nations themselves. In each situation, the actual value of M must be judged afresh, and the degree estimated to which, in that situation, potential destructive force can be realized. Naturally, the limits of relevance will vary widely, and errors in estimating them will always form one of the hazards of war. However, a constant awareness of their existence can eliminate many of the most costly and tragic errors.

There is a point, for instance, where weapons literally cease to be weapons in any contemporary context, and that without losing any of their intrinsic power to destroy. The weapons of the Civil War, the bloodiest ever fought by American forces, have lost none of their capacity for killing men. The .58 caliber musket, the cap-and-ball Colt or Remington revolver—these can still kill men as effectively as they could a hundred years ago, but no one in his right mind today thinks of them seriously as weapons. Under Federal law and the laws of most States, they are not even classed as firearms. Their value in any normal military equation is nil.

There are situations, too, where the low vulnerability of a target renders certain types of force totally irrelevant. (Presumably light fieldpieces by the thousands could be squibbed off at Gibraltar indefinitely without discommoding its garrison.) Then there are occasions—of which the Kaiser War provides innumerable sad examples—when potential destructive force is rendered irrelevant by its vulnerability during a preparatory phase necessary to its expression. Finally, there are times when force can be expressed very dramatically and with great intensity without being especially relevant to the military equation concerned; much "strategic bombardment" has been of this nature, largely because the theorists of "air power" have frequently been inclined to mistake devastation for military effectiveness.

This whole question of relevance may seem absurdly obvious, but it cannot be too strongly emphasized—especially in an age when today's industrial laser may be tomorrow's death ray, today's armor tomorrow's cardboard, today's aircraft tomorrow's swatted fly. Under these conditions, operating (whenever possible) within the limits of relevance is a primary law of military survival and military accomplishment. Beyond these limits, M, as a valid factor in the military equation, can scarcely be said to exist.

The
Expression
of M

The obvious physical determinants of force are neither the sole, nor the absolute determinants of M. Each weapon—each instrument of destructive force—has its intrinsic potentials for intensity, frequency, and radius of expression. Similarly, every instrumentality of force—every military agency which employs weapons or enables their employment—has comparable potentials deriving from these weapons and from special characteristics of its own.

Let us consider weapons first. Every weapon has an immediate radius of expression—the distance within which it can effectively strike a blow. With a sword, mace, or stabbing spear, this means the length of the weapon plus the length of the user's arm. With projectile weapons, it means the distance to which a velite can propel his javelin, a bow its arrow, a catapult its stone or dead horse or returning enemy ambassador, an arquebus its ball, an artillery piece its shot or shell, and an ICBM its warhead. Within this periphery, certain weapons have a secondary radius of expression. For shrapnel, this was a cone. For fragmenting projectiles, it is an area of impact probability and/or blast intensity; for gas shells, a zone of molecular dispersion. For nuclear weapons, the same principle applies—only more impressively.

Every weapon, too, has what may be called its *sphere of saturation*—that area over which its destructive potential is, or in a given time will be, fully realized. The time necessary for this realization will, for all practical purposes, range from zero to infinity, and will of course help to measure the relevance of the force involved.

So much for the instruments. Each instrumentality may also be said to have its *radius of expression,* throughout which, in a given time, it can perform its function of enabling weapons to perform theirs. Here again, we can distinguish between a primary radius of movement "out of action," and a secondary radius of movement "in action." (Generally speaking, such traditional terms as "strategic mobility" and "tactical mobility" tend to confuse past practice with underlying principle in the expression of destructive force.)

At any rate, there are five phases in the expression of M, throughout each of which the equations of war apply:

1. *Preparation.* Industrial production, organization, training.
2. *Logistics.* Movement "out of action."
3. *Maneuver.* Movement "in action."
4. *Weapons, primary* radius of expression.
5. *Weapons, secondary* radius of expression.

"Logistics" and "maneuver" are of course terms of convenience, imprecise and often overlapping; each is part and parcel of the same great process, and there is nothing to be gained by quibbling over where one ends and the other begins. Determinants in each phase are *time* and *maintenance,* both of which will be more fully considered later.

Bear in mind that each phase is simply a stage in a continuous single process—the expression of destructive force in the equations of war.

On any military map, one can sweep a circle showing the primary radius of expression of a rifle, a trench mortar, a howitzer. One can extend this laterally to depict the immediate scope of multiples of these weapons. Then, adding the factor of time for movement, one can draw new circles showing potential areas of expression for their instrumentalities in the logistics and maneuver phases. These figures will differ widely for every weapon and every agency of expression or maintenance, infantry or cavalry or tanks, trucks or trains, field hospitals, airfields in embryo. Their actual forms will be determined to a great extent by the terrain, which will make them circles in time rather than on the ground—for here the one-hour radius may extend fifty yards, and there as many miles. They can be beautifully demonstrated in the simplicities of naval warfare, especially since the end of the age of sail. On land, even in the most complex, difficult terrain, their careful study would make it infinitely easier to distinguish between the probable and the improbable, the attainable and the utterly unattainable.

The Geometry of War

We can invent whatever terms we choose to describe these various phases and areas of expression. Generally, the terms employed are those to which reference has already been made; however, in order to elaborate and perhaps clarify the argument, it may be useful to examine two terms which have lost much of their meaning in our contemporary context—"tactical" and "strategic."

They are loose terms; their meaning changes with the context and the user. Farrow[1] defined tactics and strategy as follows:

---

[1] Farrow, Edward S., *A Dictionary of Military Terms*, New York, Crowell, 1918.

> *Strategy.* The science of military command, and directing military movements: the use of stratagem or artifice for the carrying out of any project: the application of the broad fundamental principles of the art of war.
>
> *Tactics.* The methods employed in handling troops, in battle or in immediate preparation therefor.

These are wide nets, through which much wind has blown—until today most news media and most public men employ the words with so little precision that one can be substituted for the other without much loss of meaning. Examples of this are rather easier to find than to avoid. Even when some sort of definition is inadvertently mentioned, one is compelled to wonder how it is derived and what it means militarily. Herman Kahn,[2] for example, at one point refers to "the classical notion of 'strategy' as an attempt to force one's will on the enemy."

As it does help to set certain limits of meaning within which a discussion will begin, instead of starting with the now commonly accepted usages, let us commence with Clausewitz's definition: ". . . Tactics *teaches the use of the armed forces in engagments,* and strategy *the use of engagements to attain the object of the war.*"[3]

This is admirably precise when we apply it to Hannibal in Italy or Scipio in Spain, to the terrible onslaughts of the Mongols, to Gustavus or Turenne, to Marlborough, Saxe, or Frederick—in short, to relatively small forces armed with weapons possessing restricted radii of expression and operating over relatively large spaces. We read of Marathon and Cannae, of Bosworth Field and Malplaquet, Rossbach and Jena, Trenton and Gettysburg, and we know what *battle* means. We read of Caesar and Napoleon, and we

---

[2] Kahn, *op. cit.,* p. 163.

[3] Clausewitz, Karl von, *On War,* New York, Modern Library, 1943, p. 62.

have no doubts about the meaning of *campaign.* In the traditional battle, the mobility-in-battle of forces engaged is of the same order as the mobility-out-of-battle of those not engaged. The battle, therefore, is essentially self-limiting, for infantry and cavalry a day's march away cannot affect a decision which may be achieved by half a day's—or half an hour's—movement of the same arms on the battlefield.

Consider the simple geometry of our areas of expression. Give Brown Bess an effective radius of, say, a hundred or two hundred yards. Give her accompanying cannon a few times as much. Then consider the time necessary to move infantry, artillery, lancers and hussars, first over three or four square miles of battlefield—and then enroute to it, cross country or over wretched roads. We find the battle isolated, in space by distance, in time by the certainty of its own short duration.

How very clear the old terms, as defined by Clausewitz, are in this context. We can start Prince Eugene off from Vienna to the Rhine, and we can speak sensibly of his potentialities in terms of strategy and tactics. Then, if we begin to speak in terms of military equations, we can still label the equations "tactical" or "strategic," and we can project the various areas of expression of the diverse forces at his disposal in these terms. However, if we once take into consideration the four essential factors of the military equation, if we include the element of time as their absolute determinant—sometimes as multiplier, sometimes as divisor—then we can discard the traditional terms entirely and still make sense.

Today, we *must.*

The geometry of war has not changed. The equations of war have not changed. But the values involved have changed so drastically, and *are changing* so drastically, that we cannot afford to use terms which are no longer accurately descriptive.

The Expansion of the Battle

Very briefly, let us consider an outstanding example of the failure to think in terms of the essential equations and their values, and of the imposition of outdated frames of reference on situations to which they were not relevant—the World War I Western Front.

By 1914, the potentials of destructive force of the projectile weapons used had risen enormously. The primary and secondary areas of expression of destructive force had expanded dramatically; so had its intensity and volume. As a consequence, its areas of saturation and near-saturation were vastly greater than ever before. At the same time, the vulnerability of the soldier was as high as it had ever been, while his mobility in battle had dropped sharply because infantry could not move economically in areas of saturation and near-saturation, and cavalry, for all practical purposes, could not move at all anywhere near the battle. But railroads, and to a lesser degree motor vehicles, had multiplied mobility out of battle ten or twenty-fold.

Now, the major goal of generalship is, and has always been, to set up *un*balanced military equations—where V will be as low as possible, and M as high; where V′ will be as high as possible, and M′ as low. Naval warfare offers a perfect example in the maneuver of "crossing the T." So, on land, did Scipio's three double envelopments at Ilipa, Baecula and Zama.[4] So, in amphibious warfare, did the Inchon Landings. In the campaign, this of course involved such matters as forcing a choice of ground, destroying the source or interdicting the maintenance of force, preventing

---

[4] Liddell Hart, *Captain Sir* Basil, *A Greater Than Napoleon: Scipio Africanus,* Edinburgh and London, William Blackwood & Sons Ltd., 1930.

enemy concentrations, etc., etc. In the battle, if no major concentrations of vulnerability presented themselves, it involved the deliberate expression of force for the purpose of creating them—the crushing of a flank to enable envelopment, the breaking of a battle line for the same purpose or in order to dislocate an enemy and prevent him from achieving something similar. Always the element of time had to be brief enough to prevent the enemy from restoring the equation to its balance or, indeed, changing it in his own favor. Here cavalry and horse artillery came into their own, as did mobile infantry, and the capacity for swift decision and resolute action.

The Western Front of the First War was in no sense a campaign. Nor was it a sequence of campaigns. It was a battle—along a battle line as much as three hundred miles long, stretching from Switzerland to the Lowland Sea—a battle lasting more than four years. It was a battle with its dimensions hideously distorted, where any major fracture, any major dislocation, could be achieved only after long preparation and at vast expense; where—until the invention of the tank, which was itself not adequately exploited —nothing existed capable of the traditional swift exploitation; where out-of-battle mobility allowed every break to be repaired, every penetration to be stopped short of the decisive point. It was at once a battle and a mutual siege, the monstrous offspring of new technologies and military anachronism. In one way only did it resemble the traditional campaign—in the necessity for prolonged maintenance.

This expansion of the battle was perceived by few and understood by almost none. Commandant J. Colin,[5] then of the Ecole de Guerre, recognized some aspects of it, when he wrote, in 1911:

---

[5] Colin, *Commandant J.*, *The Transformations of War*, London, Hugh Rees Ltd., 1912, pp. 330, 331.

The battle was formerly independent of the operations: since Napoleon's day it has been intimately linked up with the operations; it now absorbs nearly all the operations.

But its most important aspects the true strength of the defensive and the utter lack of mobility in battle, he failed to see:

> Following a natural law, recent industrial and military progress has favored the defensive in frontal fights; but the offensive is more potent in imposing battle and in forcing decisions to one's advantage, *for the assailing army occupies the whole theatre of operations and sweeps all away in its passage.* [Italics added.]

Almost the only man who did accurately foretell the course of events was the Polish-Jewish banker and intellectual, I. S. Bloch,[6] who in six volumes published just before the turn of the century prophesied not only the military stalemate, but also many of its economic, social, and political consequences. Bloch's cardinal error was idealism; he believed that wars had become so terrible and so costly that men, for practical reasons, would give up fighting them.

Actually, any war or any phase of a war fought along an uninterrupted line intercepting the entire available area must, in traditional terms, be considered as a single battle. With the one exception of maintenance, previously noted, the equations ruling it will more closely approximate the equations of the battle than those of the campaign, and its historical counterparts will be found especially in those "Classic" battles where armies based themselves on fortified camps. Today the fortified camp is the nation, or half the nation. Under these circumstances, a reasonably swift

---

[6] Bloch, I. S., *The Future of War. . . . ,* Boston, Ginn & Co., (C. 1899).

decision can ordinarily be achieved only when new, less vulnerable, more mobile agencies for the expression of M— such as major armored and motorized elements, airborne troops, and carefully co-ordinated aviation—can be brought in, as they sometimes were in World War II, to redress the balance between the logistics and maneuver phases, between mobility out of action and mobility in action.

All in all, our understanding of new technological values and new military situations as they develop would be clearer were we to abandon such terms as campaign and battle, strategy and tactics, and evaluate the processes of war in terms of their equations, which can describe them much more accurately. One is, naturally, tempted to redefine the traditional terms, in the hope of restoring to them some measure of the precise meanings they had in Clausewitz's day, and of making them once again functionally applicable. But why bother? Once meanings have become obscured and distorted, once words have been rendered virtually meaningless, their continued use will breed confusion despite any attempts at redefinition—if for no other reason, then because those who use them will too often have seen them erroneously employed.

The Physical Determinants of M

In any of the equations of war, the physical determinants of M are:

1. *Weapons*, the means for expressing destructive force.
2. *Instrumentalities*, the agencies which enable that expression.
3. *Relevance*, of weapons and instrumentalities.

4. *Space,* over which force is expressed in its several phases.
5. *Time,* during which destructive force is expressed in these several phases.
6. *Maintenance,* which enables the continued expression of destructive force.

In addition, M will be influenced by V, since the vulnerability factor, when realized, can determine the rate of deterioration, and the consequent future values, of M.

The value of *weapons* as a determinant of M derives, of course, from their characteristics—their primary and secondary radii of expression, their volume of expression, their potential areas of saturation. M cannot be realized until weapons are in a position to express it. There can be no true substitute for weapons and weapon power. Sometimes, of course, skill in war can so dispose deficient force that a less able enemy will be prevented from taking advantage of his weapons superiority; and again, such an enemy may be deluded into believing that no deficiency exists. However, while these are methods always to be aimed at, they cannot be relied on to compensate for weapons deficiencies.

The value of *instrumentalities* is similarly determined by such characteristics as their ability to move, their ability to sustain the expression of force, their own vulnerability. The instrumentalities themselves do not express M, except in those now rare instances where, as in ramming at sea or in the shock employment of cavalry, the instrumentality itself becomes the weapon. Instead, they enable its expression in the weapon phases. The fact that occasionally the threat of that expression may be enough to unbalance the equation does not alter the basic physical importance of weapons potential.

Relevance has already been discussed.

The value of *space* and *time* can scarcely be considered separately, for space, in almost every phase and situation, can be a limiting determinant of time, and time, under certain circumstances, can be a limiting determinant of space. In any case, ultimately the value of space translates into a time value, only then becoming an actual operative factor in the equation itself, multiplying and/or dividing M and M', V and V'.

The value of *maintenance,* and of all the operations necessary to it through each of the several preliminary phases of expression, is determined by one thing and one only: the degree to which it enables the realization of M in the weapons phases. This decides both its positive and its negative value in the equations of war, as we shall see presently. Actually, while it is convenient to consider maintenance separately as a function, it cannot be divorced from the instrumentalities which perform it. The vulnerability of maintenance is *their* vulnerability, and theirs is its contribution to M.

As for *vulnerability,* its influence on the equations in any phase will also be measured by the ultimate effect of its realization by the enemy on the weapons phases of M, and will be determined by the degree to which its inherent potential value is so realized. In any of the phases of expression, the character of the instrumentalities involved will, naturally, determine that potential value.

Any discussion of these physical determinants of M, however brief, must include some mention of the two factors of *terrain* and *mobility.* The terms *space* and *time* apply to the abstract equations which describe the military reality; *terrain* and *mobility* are aspects of that reality which determine the value of these factors.

By determining the situational value of space, *terrain* affects the force which can be expressed over that space in any given period of time and during any of the four military phases of expression. It is a determinant, also, of the relevance of force, stating which weapons and instrumentalities will function and which will not. Indirectly, as a determinant of vulnerability, it decides the rate of attrition of force in any situation.

Mobility, on the other hand, is a determinant of *scope*, of radius of expression in the second and third phases. It is, in principle, nothing more nor less than a substitute for projectiles of unlimited range and perfect accuracy. That is its end-all and be-all. Mobility is a divisor of time in the military equation during those phases when time multiplies vulnerability and does not, as in the fourth and fifth phases, multiply destructive force.

In each and every situation, then, we find that the physical determinants of M dictate its maximum limits of realization—limits which cannot be extended without first changing the values of those determinants themselves. Actually, these limits are seldom attained, or even approached, in war. How many armies have achieved the *full* potential of the longbow, or of the high-velocity repeating rifle? How many have, like the Mongols, come close to the absolute physical limits of cavalry? How many generals have been able to utilize the force at their disposal to the ultimate of its capacity?

The Non-Physical Determinants of M

The value of the mental and moral determinants* of M *cannot* be exaggerated—but, paradoxically, it *has* been woefully exaggerated since the dawn of military history.

Everyone is familiar with such maxims as Napoleon's,

---

* NOTE. In addition to *morale* and *training*, discussed here, see also (on page 126) a discussion of a third non-physical determinant, *intellect*. See also page 129 for a further elaboration of this important non-physical determinant in achieving (or preventing) a critical imbalance.

"The moral is to the physical as three to one"—which can indeed typify them all. Nobody can deny that it is a noble sentiment, which has undoubtedly done much to hearten commanders threatened by superior forces. There is, nonetheless, one trouble with it. Taken literally, it is false.

Morale, however high, and training, however excellent, do not *multiply* destructive force. They cannot increase the value of M beyond the physical potential dictated by its other determinants. At the best, they can enable its full realization; at the worst—and herein lies their full importance—they can reduce that value cataclysmically. Their maximum mathematical value as multipliers in the military equation is therefore exactly *one*.

"How many things apparently impossible have nevertheless been performed by resolute men who had no alternative but death!" So said Napoleon,[7] and it is interesting to note two qualifications in his statement, for he speaks of the *apparently* impossible and of men who have no less desperate military alternative. *No one*, in war, has ever accomplished the impossible, but many men have accomplished that which appeared to be impossible according to accepted rules and usages, or military equations inaccurately evaluated. The line between the improbable and the physically impossible is at times a hazardous and narrow one, and in critical cases a hair's breadth appears to divide victory from defeat, success from senseless suicide. Actually, when all values in the equation concerned become apparent, this is less frequently found to be the case.

No amount of military enthusiasm can increase the cyclic rate of fire of a machine gun, or make a machine gun out of a matchlock musket, or take a half-track over bad terrain at ten times the speed machine and terrain together dictate.

---

[7] Phillips, *Major* Thomas R. (ed.), *Roots of Strategy*, Harrisburg, Pa., Military Service Pub. Co., 1941.

No amount of courage can make swords and bayonets anything more than long knives with handles and shorter knives on sticks, or diminish the vulnerability of the people handling them, or keep armies forever fighting on when maintenance is nonexistent, or compensate for vastly superior force exercised by men equally well trained and resolute.

This does not mean that "inferior" force should never try its strength against "superior." It does not mean that Sir James Scarlett's Heavy Brigade should not repeatedly have charged vastly larger Russian elements at Balaklava; nor that John Paul Jones should have surrendered *Bonhomme Richard;* nor that the Battle of Britain should not have been fought against the Luftwaffe.

But it does mean that Marshal Ney should not have persisted in sacrificing his massed cavalry at Waterloo; that poor Rozhdestvensky had no chance at all when he tried to force Tsushima Straits; that, for all practical military purposes, Japan's *kamikaze* pilots in the last phase of the Pacific war should not have attempted their suicidal attacks on U.S. naval vessels.

There are—and while men fight there always will be—occasions when the impossible *must* be attempted. But military doctrine should not prescribe the attempting of it as a matter of routine. In the equations of war, and especially in a technological age, heroism—vital as it is—is no adequate *substitute* either for hardware or horse sense.

The Evaluation of M

It will at once be obvious, of course, that M cannot be evaluated properly in isolation, in terms of destructive force alone, and that to attempt this can often be to court disaster. Regardless of whether the problem of evaluation comprehends one, two, or more of the phases of expression of force, *all* the determinants of M must be considered.

This is true even of so simple a business as a fire fight between two companies of infantry or an action between two surface fleets. It is even more emphatically true in operations involving numerous dissimilar instrumentalities. Where the possible survival of nations is concerned, it becomes critical.

It is interesting, in this latter context, to compare the speeches of General Tojo and of Admiral Nomura, delivered when the Japanese offensive in the Pacific and in Asia had reached its limits of success. Tojo, who understood neither the United States nor our Allies, boasted without qualification that Japan's victory had been won and the "Greater East Asia Co-Prosperity Sphere" securely established. Nomura, a far more sophisticated man, claimed nothing of the sort; as I recall, he simply prayed for a possible eventual victory.

Certainly, Tojo was not the only man who overestimated the destructive force at the disposal of the Axis in 1942, or who underestimated that which could rapidly be developed by the United States. It is extremely easy, and extremely tempting, to believe in one's own absolute superiority, and, so believing, to mistake one aspect of the military process for its entirety. While the tendency to do so can perhaps be encouraged as a virtue in sergeants, it can only be deplored as a vice in Commanders-in-Chief and Ministers of State.

M must inevitably be evaluated as one factor, *and one only*, of the equations of war. It must be reëvaluated at every stage and for every new situation. This does not mean that at each juncture the obvious must be slowly and precisely measured, that "time out" must be taken to prove again that which has been already proven. It simply means that, when changes have taken place in the determinants of M or V, M' or V', they must always be allowed for. The whole equation must always be borne in mind.

Indeed, it might not be a bad idea to provide for this in basic staff organization on various levels, designating appropriate personnel for the evaluation of each of the four basic factors in the equation. This would provide some insurance against the overlooking of any one of them, especially in those perilous situations where a single unperceived or unanticipated value change can throw the whole equation out of balance. It would make certain that functional evaluation and revaluation of the military process would be continuous throughout its duration.

The Escalation of Destructive Force

The central characteristic of warfare in our time is the technological escalation of destructive force. One aspect of this has already been discussed—the expansion of the battle, involving a gross imbalance between the second and third phases in the expression of M, especially those factors of M comprehending the movement of the instrumentalities. Even more impressive, however, has been the effect on the two final phases, the primary and secondary weapons phases.

If we plot curves to illustrate the development of weapons since the Renaissance, we find that in every phase (though by no means uniformly in all phases) the curves—like most curves depicting scientific progress—follow a geometrical progression, becoming steeper and steeper until now, in the second half of the Twentieth Century, in the two final phases some of them appear to be reaching asymptote.

Take the artillery curve from Mons Meg on—through the clumsy siege guns of the Thirty Years War, the Parrott rifles of the War Between The States, the railroad guns and primitive bombers of World War I, the Flying Fortresses and rockets of World War II, into the age of modern ballistic missiles with hydrogen warheads. Two curves can be drawn for this purpose—one illustrating primary radii of expression; the other, secondary. Neither needs describing. Both are equally impressive.

Here we find the first three phases in the expression of M (Preparation, Logistics and Maneuver) virtually eliminated from consideration—the first because full weaponry will already have been prepared and situated prior to war; the second and third, because the expansion of the fourth (Weapons, primary radius) and fifth (Weapons, secondary radius of expression) renders them unnecessary. No longer can any full-scale war—that is to say, any war with all restraints removed—be a pavane of strategy and tactics, marches and countermarches, penetrations and envelopments. Technology, by expanding the two final areas of expression *and of saturation,* has decreed that such a war will be fundamentally an artillery problem. Its weapons, whatever we care to call them, are artillery weapons. Its equations are the equations of artillery. Peripheral weapons may play a part in such a war, but that part can scarcely be a decisive one—unless, of course, new and radically different weapons and counter weapons emerge unexpectedly from what now appears to be the periphery.

[In the November-December 1968 issue of *Ordnance,* published while this book was undergoing a final revision, there appeared an article entitled "Tactical Nuclear Combat," by the well-known writer and historian, Colonel T. N. Dupuy. In developing his thesis—which need not concern us at this point—Colonel Dupuy referred to a study prepared for the United States Army by the Historical Evaluation and Research Organization (HERO) in October 1964, under the title "Historical Trends Related to Weapon Lethality," which in turn was based on a practical and imaginative approach proposed by Major William C. Stewart, C.C. in an earlier article, "Interaction of Firepower, Mobility, and Dispersion," published in the March 1960 *Military Review*.

Colonel Dupuy reproduced three tables from the HERO study. Two of these are so interesting and so immediately pertinent to the immediate argument that they are shown here. Despite the fact that they do not distinguish between the weapons phases in the expression of destructive force, they do illustrate very clearly the effect of weapons development and of increased mobility on destructive force and on dispersion:

Weapons	*Lethality Index*
Hand-to-hand (sword, pike, etc.)	20
Javelin	18
Ordinary bow	20
Longbow	34
Crossbow	32
Arquebus	10
17th century musket	19
18th century flintlock	47
Early 19th century rifle	36
Mid-19th century rifle (conoidal bullet)	154
Late 19th century breech-loading rifle	229
Springfield Model 1903 rifle (magazine)	778
World War I machine gun	12,730
World War II machine gun	17,980
16th century 12-pounder cannon	43
17th century 12-pounder cannon	229
Gribeauval 18th century 12-pounder cannon	3,970

French 75-mm. gun	340,000
155-mm. GPF	474,000
155-mm. "Long Tom"	533,000
105-mm. howitzer, M1	644,000
World War I tank	68.300
World War II medium tank	2,203,000
World War I fighter-bomber	229,200
World War II fighter-bomber	3,037,900
V-2 ballistic missile	861,000
20-kiloton nuclear air burst	48,550,000
One-megaton nuclear air burst	661,500,000

I. *Theoretical lethality indices for selected weapons.*

Item	Napoleonic Wars	Civil War	World War I	World War II	1970?
Area of 100,000 men (sq. miles)	8.05	10.3	99	1,290	33,500
Average frontage of 100,000 men (miles)	5.7	6.4	9	34	160
Average depth of 100,000 men (miles)	1.4	1.6	11	38	209
Average diagonal for 100,000 men (miles)*	5.9	6.6	14.2	51	264
Lethality index totals (in millions)	5.5	14.3	232.8	1,280.5	32,500
Movement rate for major reserves (m.p.h.)**	2	2	2	15	x***
Time to cross diagonal (hours)	2.95	3.3	7.1	3.4	y***

* Maximum distance from which reserves could be committed within the area of sector.

** For the Napoleonic, Civil, and First World Wars, major reserves within the sector of a 100,000-man force were committed on foot, at an average rate of 2 m.p.h. For World War II, major reserves were committed within such a sector by truck, at an average rate of 15 m.p.h. For a future war in 1970, see note below.

*** If x is 25, y is 10.5; if x is 50, y is 5.3; if x is 60, y is 4.4.

II. *Basic lethality, dispersion, and mobility factors.*

The values these tables give may or may not be precisely accurate. That is unimportant. They are accurate enough so that we should bear them in mind whenever we consider the development of M over the past and the future, and whenever we try, in the light of that continuing development, to estimate what M must become in the not-too-distant future, and what effect its escalation may have on specific military equations, on any or all of their possible factors, on wars of every sort, and on human survival.]

Regrettably, at this point we must return once more to Herman Kahn and his Doomsday Machines. He lists three types: the Doomsday Machine, the Doomsday-in-a-Hurry Machine, and the Homicide Pact Machine (which isn't quite a Doomsday Machine)—the unpleasant details of which we need not harp on. As a firm believer only in the intelligent, efficient, and restrained use of force for civilized purposes—and my definition of these terms more closely resembles those of the Eighteenth and Nineteenth Centuries than it does today's—I must confess that I am horrified by the *sang froid* with which Mr. Kahn and so many of his colleagues discuss these matters. As he steps from one imaginary hecatomb to another, he does pause occasionally to reassure us:

> I have been surprised at the unanimity with which the notion of the unacceptability of a Doomsday Machine is greeted. I used to be wary of discussing the concept for fear that some colonel would get out a General Operating Requirement or Development Planning Objective for the device, but it seems that I need not have worried. Except by some scientists and engineers who have overemphasized the single objective of maximizing the effectiveness of deterrence, the device is universally rejected. It just does not look professional to senior officers, and it looks even worse to senior civilians. *The fact that more than a few scientists and engineers do seem attracted to the idea is disquieting,* [Italics mine.—R.B.] *but as long as the development*

project is expensive, even these dedicated experts are un-likely to get one under way.[8]

Who has ever met a colonel who would seriously con-sider blowing up the world in a game of "chicken"? Even that poor benighted heathen, Genghis Khan, limited his genocide to those peoples who either resisted him or were, in his opinion, taking up good grazing land. He, of course, did not have the excuse of "pure science," so often used to-day to relieve the scientist from all responsibility for his contrivances. The professional soldier enjoys no such im-munity; nor can he so simply (except perhaps in Marxist countries, where he officially doesn't have one) shrive his soul—and this may be why Herman Kahn encountered such reluctance to accept what any civilized soldier must—from both a moral and a military standpoint—reject out of hand.

May it be that the world stands in far greater danger from the scientist than from the soldier? During World War II, I worked for a Federal agency which found it nec-essary to bring people of little previous consequence—as "area experts"—into positions where they could get a taste of swaying great affairs. Megalomania grows fantastically in such a climate; and this may be what has happened to some scientists. Their new-found power and importance is too much for them. No dictator, no insane fanatic holding authority, has ever lacked for scientists to do his work—even to "prove" the most unscientific of his theories—at least while he could frighten them, or pay them well, or offer them prestige. Some have withdrawn quietly into obscure alcoves of research; some have defected; a few have paid for their defiance with their lives. But even more have been good dogs. What defense does the world have today, in its crazy anarchy of a hundred and a quarter sovereign na-

---

[8] Kahn, *op. cit.*, p. 148.

tions, some of them not yet emerged from savagery, against mad leadership and its hired or terrorized scientific servants?

Let us close this discussion with one more Herman Kahn quotation:

> . . . It is my belief that neither the U.S. nor the Soviet Union will manufacture any Doomsday Machines, but this will be a political, economic, and moral choice and not one dictated by technology. (I should add that I hold this belief only moderately firmly.) The year 1973 may be a bit early to see the possibility that any of twenty nations will have the capability to manufacture Doomsday Machines, but we have been surprised before at the rate of technological development.[9]

After this chapter, it will be refreshing to return, even though perhaps uncomforted, to a healthier area of human intellectual activity, the consideration of more or less limited war, where the enthusiasm of the dedicated experts can (hopefully) be held in check either by frightened statesmen or by the good sense of the military.

The Automation of Destructive Force

The automation of war, through every phase of the expression of destructive force, is probably as inevitable as the automation of industry, and, like that social phenomenon, is already something of a *fait accompli*. In many areas, where we have become used to the replacement of men by machines, we scarcely notice it. Nobody stops to think that a machine gun replaces quite a number of rifleman; that

---

[9] *Ibid.* p. 510.

one large truck with a single driver replaces several horse-drawn wagons with their complement of personnel; that a single chain saw can take the place of a whole squad of pioneers, and one small steam engine that of a hundred galley slaves.

"Automation" has been with us a long time. However, it is only recently—and again because of the accelerating curve of scientific progress—that we have had to name it. It started with machines replacing muscle power. It continued with their taking over certain of the simpler directive functions. First came the man doing the work with the tool, then the tool doing the work under the man's guidance, then another tool—the "computer"—guiding various tools throughout an entire complex operation. Once the machine has been developed to the point where it can perform any of these functions reliably, it is in all ways *but one* superior to a man. It is far simpler than a man structurally. Once developed, it takes less time and effort to produce. It is easier to understand, to program, to predict. It is usually less vulnerable, or at least less *generally* vulnerable. Its physical limitations are not rigidly set by nature, and therefore may be extended more or less indefinitely through re-design. Its problems of supply and repair are ordinarily much simpler. Besides, it asks neither for pay nor leave, requires no recreational facilities, and is never insubordinate —at least willfully.

There is, indeed, only one thing the machine cannot do. It cannot *think*. No machine, not even the most complex computer, really thinks. It merely extends and speeds up the thinking of the men who provide the data for it. How often, among these men, will one find a Grant, a Sherman, a Sheridan, a Nathan Bedford Forrest? There is, most decidedly, a danger in delegating too much of the computing function to machines, for under certain circumstances this could mean surrendering the power of decision to military and academic mediocrities—even to the sort of men who, preoccupied with their own pedantries, might fail to perceive either the jaws of disaster or the gates of victory.

Several factors will determine the degree of automation achieved at any given time in the various phases of expression. One will be real or apparent *military necessity*. Another will be *expense*—where the necessity seems less pressing. A third will be the *applicability* of *contemporary science* and *technology*—the state of the art. Thus, we may expect a higher rate of automation in those areas where high values or intensities of M are expressed by a relatively few powerful weapons and instrumentalities: in naval warfare, for example, or in missile and counter-missile operations, especially where militarily critical or economically vital targets are concerned.

It may be quite some time before the computer universally replaces the company commander, or the machine the mess sergeant. However, as these devices intrude more and more on man's province, a strange phenomenon will become increasingly apparent: the importance of morale will diminish, and the number of fearless and resolute men necessary to the prosecution of a war will decrease fantastically. The significance of professional armed forces will, then, rise correspondingly.

But the equations of war will still, inexorably, decide the outcome of any conflict.

Time
And The
Equations
Of War

In the equations of war, as in those describing all other processes, there is one invariant, one invariable—the flow of time. Terrain and weather and the works of man operate to alter the military value of space. Techniques of weapons employment and unit maintenance operate to determine the actual values of destructive force. But absolute time is a constant. A minute is a minute, an hour an hour, a day a day—regardless of season or locality or situation. Time, literally, is a dimension of all processes; without it process could not be. Throughout the several phases of the expression of force, the *rates* of T and T' are identical. My hour is yours; there is not a whit of difference between Wellington's and Napoleon's, Kuropatkin's and Kuroki's,

Time is the third inescapable factor in the equations of war. Throughout the several phases—preparatory, logistics, maneuver, weapons—involved in the expression of destructive force, time is an absolute determinant both of force and of realized vulnerability, sometimes as a multiplier, sometimes as a divisor. Nothing has caused the loss of so many battles, campaigns, and wars as the failure to evaluate the time factor properly. Nothing has contributed so often to decisive victory as the ability to judge it accurately.

Grant's and Lee's—and Joshua left behind no training manual to teach us differently. Therefore the genius of great captains lies not in how they manipulate this factor, but rather in how, recognizing that it cannot be manipulated, they adapt their plans and dispositions to its inflexibility.

Time and the Principles of War

It is a curious fact that, in examining the various sets of rules or principles of war, from Sun Tzu's on into modern times, we find that they deal with the element of time largely by implication, much as they deal with the equally important factor of vulnerability. This is true of Clausewitz and Jomini, writing about the formal campaigns and set-piece battles of their day, and it is equally true of those modern sets of principles already cited.

The main exception—the only formulation which, to the author's knowledge at least, does not take the element of time pretty much for granted—is the statement of what may be called "equations of mutual attrition" by F. W. Lanchester. In a work entitled *Aircraft in Warfare, the Dawn of the Fourth Arm*,[1] published during the first part of World War I, Lanchester, an aircraft engineer, set forth what he termed his N^2 *Law:* "the *fighting strength* of a force may be broadly defined as proportional *to the square of its numerical strength multiplied by the fighting value of its individual units.*"

Lanchester gave equations for finding the rate of reduction of each of two contending forces, and in these equations, of course, t was a factor. He did not allow for the negative factor of vulnerability, nor for the manifold complexities (of which he was fully aware) of land warfare. Nonetheless, his formulation may very profitably be read today, and is of special interest as applied to naval warfare in his analysis of Trafalgar—a study to which I shall give considerable space in the chapter following this one.

Time and the
Processes
of War

The processes of war are on the one hand positive, those

---

[1] Lanchester, F. W., *Aircraft in Warfare, the Dawn of the Fourth Arm*, London, Constable & Co. Ltd., 1916.

involving the expression of destructive force, and on the other negative, those involving the vulnerability of man and his works to such force expressed against him. Each military equation must comprehend, therefore, the destructive force expressed by both sides, or M and M', and the vulnerability of both sides, V and V'. Absolute time is their multiplier, the realizing factor. This holds true in every phase of the expression of destructive force: Preparation, Logistics, Maneuver, and the two Weapons phases.

T and T' can be simply defined: they represent the duration of opposing military processes, and one cannot be considered without the other. Viewed in potential, as they must always be until they become a part of military history, they can be defined as the time periods apparently necessary to the completion of any of these processes, their values being positive where M and M' are concerned and negative where V and V' are involved.

The rule that T and T' must always be considered together is of prime importance, for there is the temptation —frequent in war and even more frequent in time of peace —to proceed as though military time were "open ended" and flexible rather than a dictatorial imperative. This is especially so when no clear and present specific danger of war exists, or in a world where war is not a persisting environmental hazard. Thus, in the period between the Civil War and the Spanish-American, at least on land there seemed to be no urgent reason for the United States to exert itself in martial preparations; it did not matter very much whether a rifle to replace the trapdoor Springfiield was adopted five years earlier or five years later, whether the army had Gatling guns or did not have them. By comparison, the years from Hitler's invasion of the Rhineland to the opening of World War II showed far more clearly the inexorable passage of military time for both sides, and during the past two decades it has been only too obvious that time in the equations of war permits neither of its aspects to be ignored with impunity. The history of nations offers innumerable examples of disasters caused by the failure, of statesmen and of soldiers, to perceive this— to see that, while time itself is infinite, military time, which applies to finite processes, must be as finite as are the processes themselves.

Throughout each phase, throughout every process of war, T and T' are finite, and their duration is determined by the other factors involved: the initial factors of M and M' and V and V', then, as a result of their interaction, M→ and M'→, V→ and V'→, the arrows of course denoting the duration of the process, the time factor. In turn, T and T' are themselves determinants of the value of all these factors; if not in one phase, then in another. Thus, ammunition supply can determine the duration of an action, but the time required to bring up that ammunition can determine the character of the action or, indeed, whether it will take place at all. Similarly, a highly vulnerable instrument may possess the potential for expressing a very high value of M for a given period of time (that is, a high potential value of M→), but if its V is similarly realized (V→) then obviously it will be incapable of realizing that potential fully. The vast potential firepower of our own fleet at Pearl Harbor, or of *Repulse* and *Prince of Wales* later on, was negated in a very brief period of time by the sudden realization of their vulnerability.

The Evaluation of T and T'

The cardinal rule in evaluating the essential factors of the military equation is that none of them can be considered separately. In every instance, each and every one of them must be considered and evaluated with each other. This is particularly important where T and T′ are concerned, for the passing hours have often seemed less real than passing cannon, and the silent onset of a point in time far less menacing than the observed approach of distant armor. It is easy to forget that M→ and M′→, V→ and V′→ will be determined as absolutely by the time factor as by the count of regiments, the weight of metal, the weakness or the strength of fortresses. Therefore, no matter what the situation, no matter what difficulties beset the enemy, no matter what advantages a commander may possess, he still must keep both potential T and potential T′ in mind lest, having failed to do so, he find himself confronted by an abrupt and unanticipated change in the equation. Probably more engagements, campaigns, and wars have been lost through the failure to assess T and T′ correctly than from any errors in weighing the immediate values of vulnerability or destructive force.

Actually, in potential, T and T′ must each be considered in two situational aspects: as the time probably *required* for the expression of any desired value of M→, and, conversely, as the time probably *available* for that expression. The latter aspect will be determined by the probable values of M′→, V→, and V′→. Again, two analogous situational aspects reveal themselves in the evaluation of vulnerability potentials: the time in which a given value of V→ will probably be realized, and that probably needed for a comparable realization of V′→. It would, of course, be possible to devise a special system of notation for these values; however, that would doubtless be too formalistic, especially as the purpose here is to outline a general structural relationship rather than to set up rigid equations.

It has been stated that the time factors are equally important through all the phases of expression. However, before discussing this, it must be repeated that these phases as they have been defined herein are by no means hard and fast; they are simply more or less accurate labels of convenience, which could have been quite rigorously applied to warfare as it was in the days of the true battle and classical campaign, but which today must usually be employed more flexibly. Naturally, they overlap and merge; in wars of armed camp nations and continuous fronts, they persist simultaneously, more than ever in the past. They serve, nonetheless, as a useful framework for example and discussion, defining limits within which underlying principle may be coherently illustrated.

T and T',
the First Phase:
Preparation

The years prior to, and during, World War II provide a number of dramatic instances of the failure to assess potential T and T' in the first phase correctly. Outstanding among these is the gross Japanese overestimate of the time the United States would need, not only to recreate the destructive force lost at Pearl Harbor and elsewhere, but to bring into existence a potential $M' \rightarrow$ capable of threatening the new Japanese empire in East Asia and the South Pacific; and coupled with this, of course, was a corresponding underestimate of the time the Japanese themselves would require to consolidate that empire, exploit its vast resources, and convert them into a vastly increased potential $M \rightarrow$ of their own.

The fact that this was due in part to the Japanese military's insistence on believing their own semi-mystical propaganda and that of their Axis allies, and to the consequent underestimation of the American and Allied will to fight, does not alter the physical fact that, where the grand equation of the War was concerned, the central Japanese error was in their misjudgment of probable T and T', and therefore of ultimate M→ and M'→. A quotation from a Japanese propaganda magazine, *The New Order In Greater East Asia*, April 1942,[2] explaining "Nippon's prudent national defense policy," reveals the state of mind behind this:

> The Imperial Army, early in 1936, realized the need of drastically expanding military preparedness and the productive capacity. Noting that arms expansion and rearmament among various European powers would be completed during the period from 1940 to 1942, the Army concluded that an international crisis might occur at about that time.
>
> Planning a drastic expansion of military preparedness and the productive capacity by 1942, the Army enforced a six-year arms expansion program, extending from 1937 to 1942, and a five-year productive capacity increase plan, extending from 1937 to 1941 . . .
>
> To be more explicit, the Army devoted 40 per cent of its budget to the China Emergency while the balance of 60 per cent was appropriated for the expansion of military preparedness at home. Furthermore, the Army consumed 20 per cent of iron and other important materials supplied to it in the China Emergency; the remaining 80 per cent was used for the expansion of military preparedness.
>
> As a result, air and mechanized units were greatly expanded.
>
> The fighting power of the Imperial Army has, in all, become more than three times as strong as that before the outbreak of the China Emergency.
>
> Together with the Imperial Navy, whose strength was hardly affected by the China Emergency, the Imperial Army has consolidated the foundation for meeting any new emergency.
>
> Along with this, the capacity of the munitions industry was expanded from 700 to 800 per cent.

---

[2] Tolischus, Otto D., *Through Japanese Eyes*, New York, Reynal and Hitchcock, 1945, pp. 73-74.

There is more of this sort of stuff, but it all reduces to the simple picture of a nation with a relatively small industrial establishment geared to war, and with large and aggressive armed forces, completely misunderstanding the potential of an intended enemy whose vast industrial complex is geared to peace and whose armed forces not only are subordinate to the civil authority but (with the exception of the Navy) are embarrassingly small.

The questions facing the Japanese command were nothing so abstract as, *Will the United States fight or not? Will the United States translate its enormous industrial resources into destructive force?* They were, instead, *How long will it take the United States to accomplish this? How long will it take us to consolidate our newly gained empire and build up to their potential? How long will it be before our many vulnerability factors, at home and abroad, are realized by the enemy? How long will we require to achieve the realization of their comparable vulnerabilities?* In other words, the Japanese should have asked themselves, in terms of T and T', questions about potential M→ and M'→, V→ and V'→. Had they done so, realistically, they might have stayed at home and sensibly pursued the arts of peace.

As they eventually discovered, when you ask the wrong questions you very often get the wrong answers.

The years since Japan's surrender have seen two errors of comparable gravity in estimating T' in the first phase, but the men responsible, unfortunately, do not have the excuse of Japan's soldiers and statesmen, who were, after all, only seventy years removed from an isolated, ingrown feudalism. The mistakes in question consist first of grossly underestimating the time required by the Russians to produce fission bombs, fusion bombs, and the sophisticated delivery systems often considered necessary for their delivery, and secondly of similar errors in estimating the time needed by other formerly non-nuclear nations to do likewise. As a result of this, as well as of our own inane policy of Balkanizing the world, we now face a management problem in world affairs which will require the very active intercession of St. Jude for its solution.

T and T',
the Second Phase:
Logistics

As we have seen in this discussion of the first phase, the phases are only in one sense sequential. At one time or another, the later phases *must* be preceded by the earlier ones, which are of course prerequisite, but for many years it has been normal for all or almost all of them to proceed thenceforward simultaneously, as they did in World War I and World War II, the Russo-Japanese War, and the Civil War.

This was not always so. In the good old days, it was by no means uncommon for a prince to summon his vassals, levy a tribute on his subjects, assemble horse and foot, gather provisions and camp followers, and march bravely forth to do more or less formal, more or less decisive, battle with his neighbor. By and large, a campaign would be fought with the force available, or at least with that which could be made available without starting all over again; if it could not be, and if all was not lost, it would be broken off and taken up again after, say, next year's harvest.

The Industrial Revolution, the railroad, and motor transport changed all that. The decision now rested, not on a simple phase sequence (or perhaps on a simple complex of phase sequences), but on a continuing complexity. It is only very recently that the development of superweapons, and the consequent transformation of any major war into one vast artillery problem, has restored even more than its ancient simplicity to the military process. This will be discussed at length later; for the moment, we can pretend that it has not yet occurred, and examine the time factors of the second phase in the traditional scheme of warfare, and also in the modern context of "limited war," where that phase still plays more or less its traditional role.

The nature of the logistics phase is simple: it comprehends the movement of those instruments and instrumentalities of destructive force which otherwise could not be expressed effectively up to the areas where they can be so expressed, or, conversely, their movement from those areas of expression for use elsewhere or to avoid the realization of their vulnerability. Potential T and T′, then, during this phase represent the time required either for the completion of these movements or for the critical realization of V→.

It is difficult, today, to say where the second phase (Logistics) ends and the third (Maneuver) begins, and as a matter of fact there is no need to draw a sharp dividing line between them. It is enough for the moment to discuss examples which very clearly *do* belong to the logistics phase, and which illustrate the importance of judging potential T and T′ correctly and the consequences of failing to do so.

A classic example of the importance of T and T′ in this phase is the advantage traditionally enjoyed by a combatant operating on interior lines of communication over an opponent operating on exterior lines. The German experience in two world wars demonstrates it very clearly, and there are of course numberless other specific instances. It is important, however, to understand that sheer *distance* is not the absolute determinant in these situations; nor is the topology of the theater of war. It is the *time* required to traverse the distances involved that really counts, and every military map, at least in the imagination, should be

redrawn in its terms. A thousand miles of air, a hundred
of paved highway, fifty of open sea—all these can be
traversed in a fraction of the time required to struggle
through a mile or two of dense jungle or toil up rude tracks
over two or three miles of mountain pass. In such situations,
a combatant may appear to be operating on interior lines,
but the appearance may be utterly delusive, for the difference—*in the equation*—between interior and exterior lines
is invariably one of *time*. How, from the fall of Rome to the
rebuilding of good roads, could the kings of Europe defend
their coasts against bold raiders and bold conquerors from
the sea?

Needless to say, the rule regarding the importance of T
and T' in this phase does not apply only to interior and exterior lines. It applies universally, to every operation which
may be said to fall within the phase. Thus, the sluggard
civilizations of both East and West, from Kara Khitai to
Vienna's gates, never were able really to understand the
central reason for the success of the swift, relentless, all-
conquering Mongols, nor to protect themselves against
them. The secret was, of course, mobility—which means
nothing more nor less than the power to reduce the value of
T against a comparable and preferably unchanging value
of T'. So little was this understood that only by an act of
God—the death of Ogatai—was Europe saved from Mongol
domination.[3] So little was it understood that even later
generations failed to draw the correct theoretical conclusions from the history of the Mongol conquests. Even today
it still is very generally assumed that armies *naturally* must
consist of more and less mobile elements, so that the ultimate mobility of the army *as a whole* becomes that of its
least mobile components. The proof of this appears in the

---

[3] Prawdin, Michael, *The Mongol Empire, Its Rise and Legacy*, London,
George Allen and Unwin Ltd., 1941, p. 269.

fact that no army today—with all our engines and our sciences—can move as swiftly *as an army* as the unencumbered Mongols moved seven hundred years ago.

Before any opening of hostilities, and throughout their course, the vital importance of T and T′ in the logistics phase must be evaluated accurately and kept constantly in mind, for the history of failure in the field is only too often that of the failure or inability of commanders to appraise these factors properly. Because of this, badly needed armies —like Beauregard's, summoned too late by Lee on the eve of Gettysburg—are not where they should be at the critical moment; available time is not adequate. Because of it, situations where M is high and M′ low deteriorate until their values are more nearly balanced—which is what occurred at Gallipoli after the British landings at Suvla Bay, where their very considerable forces were initially opposed only by small Turkish units. To quote Kannengiesser Pasha:[4]

> During the whole of the 8th August the goddess of victory held the door of success wide open for Stopford, but he would not enter. He personally remained on the 8th, as on the 7th August, on board the *Jonquil*, because of the wireless and other signal communications, and only paid a visit to land in the afternoon.
>
> There everybody was busily employed. Baggage and rations for the troops were unloaded. Order was restored amongst the troops, trenches were dug, the men cooked and smoked and, as Churchill relates, bathed in the beautiful cool sea. They awaited the still missing artillery whose arrival had been delayed owing to the necessity of landing water, as thirst was heavy in the heat of those cloudless August days. But nobody advanced. In short, a peaceful picture almost like a boy scout's field day.
>
> At the same time under this same sun on the other side the panting troops of the 7th and 12th Divisions were

---

[4] Kannengiesser *Pasha*, Hans, *The Campaign in Gallipoli*, London, Hutchinson & Co. Ltd., 1928.

straining forward over the hills from Bulair; from the Asiatic side along the shadeless Sultan's Way; over Erenkoi the Turkish battalions and batteries were pressing towards the embarcation stations in Tchanak Kale . . .

The result? The heights, the strong positions which the Australians should immediately have seized to open the way for the exploitation of their landings and to prevent the enemy from exploiting the concentration of vulnerability which their beachhead constituted, were seized by Turks instead. The rest is history.

Mobility and the Time Factor

The entire question of mobility and its role as a determinant of T and T′ in the equations of the second and third phases is so very interesting that we will now digress, dropping the specific discussion of the phases themselves for the moment in order to examine more closely the matter of mobility.

It would seem, at first glance, that mobility would require no definition. Webster tells us that it is the ". . . Capacity or facility of movement . . ." which certainly seems simple enough. Yet militarily we must immediately distinguish between an intrinsic capacity for movement and the situational ability to realize that capacity. Here mobility is only an absolute factor in potential—infantry potentially can march so many miles a day, cavalry so many more, siege trains so many the less. In the realization, mobility is always relative; regardless of its potential value, its actual value is determined also by the mobility of the enemy. Just as it itself is a determinant of T and T′, so is its realized value a function of M and M′, V and V′.

As a determinant of time in the equations of war, mobility also becomes a determinant of realized M→. More mobile elements can build up M faster than less mobile ones; they can maintain M more readily; they can express M over a greater radius, and do so with greater frequency. The limitations are technological: do the means for rapid movement exist? can they be adapted to all weapons? how will their employment affect vulnerability?

In short, while sometimes increased mobility may seem worthless or even detrimental, this is not true in principle, for—unless the means used to achieve it are themselves too vulnerable, too expensive, or too difficult to maintain— the ability to move more rapidly than the enemy must always be an advantage. Almost universally, however, our attitudes toward mobility in war have been conditioned by accustomed usage, by forms adopted long ago, by our cultural traditions. We have considered it in these terms rather than in the more basic terms of the equations of war. For centuries, for example, armies have consisted of infantry, cavalry, and artillery, and consequently we find statements such as this, by tank pioneer Lieutenant-General Sir Giffard Martel:[5]

> Although we were limited to these slow tanks for most of the [First World] war we saw quite clearly that we needed two types of tank. Armies had always been divided into two types of troops. There were the fast mobile troops whose duty it was to feel out and find the enemy and work round his flanks and attack him where he was weak. This work had always been done by light cavalry. Then there were the slower moving, harder hitting troops whose duty it was to hold or break through strong positions. These troops had always been infantry formations. Both these types of troops needed assistance from the tanks. Fast and

---

[5] Martel, *Lt. Gen. Sir Giffard, The Problem of Security,* London, Michael Joseph Ltd., 1945, p. 109.

less heavily armoured tanks were needed to help the mobile troops corresponding to the light cavalry, and heavier but slower tanks were needed to help the infantry corresponding to heavy cavalry in the past. This became our definite policy and we had both these types of tanks before the war ended.

It does not matter that this statement may have been factually correct with regard to the types of tanks required or the functions they performed. The important thing is that it sounds as though they were required to perform them *because* various types of infantry and cavalry had performed them in the past. Thus an accurate analogy is transformed, intentionally or not, into an entirely inaccurate cause-and-effect relationship.

Even J. F. C. Fuller seems to accept the assumption that the traditional order of armies derives from the natural laws of war. In *Foundations of the Science of War*,[6] having defined "tactical action" as "protected *organized* movement through offensive action," he goes on to say.

> To accomplish this we require three orders of troops. Troops which will protect the attackers, troops which can attack, and troops which can pursue. These three orders remain fundamental, and to pull their full weight they must co-operate—that is, work together to attain a common object.
>
> In a present-day army these orders are represented by artillery, infantry, and cavalry . . .

Now, it seems that these orders of troops have been necessary to the performance of these functions only because technology and the state of the military art have seldom enabled one order of troops to perform them all, and that these techno-cultural limitations on the ability to

---

[6] Fuller, *op. cit.*, p. 171.

express M→ have therefore been accepted much too uncritically. In *principle*, there is no reason whatsoever why an army should consist of *more* and *less* mobile elements, nor why all its combat elements should not be able to perform all its functions. In practice, naturally, there have almost always been insuperable obstacles to the achievement of this ideal, but the one exception in which the ideal was realized—again, the armies of the Mongols—teaches us that it is well worth bearing in mind as long as war remains part of our existence.

Liddell Hart perceived this forty years ago when, writing of the Mongols, he declared:[7]

> The prime feature of the Mongol military system was therefore its simplicity, due to the use of a single arm, in contrast to the inevitably complex organization of a combination of several arms which has always characterized European armies. In this way the Mongols solved the ever-difficult problem of co-operation between arms which have radically different qualities and limitations. The single arm they used was that which possessed the highest degree of mobility, and in this lay the secret of their unbroken run of victory.

It is interesting to compare the mobility of the Mongols in both the second and third phases with the mobility of armies since their time. In its January 1964 issue, the *Military Review* published the digest of an article by Captain H. H. Montfort of the Swiss Army, under the title, "The Blitzkrieg Myth."[8] In it, the author sought to prove that modern mechanized forces had restored mobility in the field only to the level attained in pre-mechanized times,

---

[7] Liddell Hart, *Captain Sir* Basil, *Great Captains Unveiled*, Boston, Little Brown & Co., 1928, p. 32.

[8] *Military Review*, Vol. XLIV, No. I, January 1964, pp. 71-73.

and cited a number of examples in support of this contention. Among these were the following:

Operation	Days	Miles	Average
1940 German campaign in France	35	220	6.28
1941 German attack on Russia	176	600	3.15
1942 Rommel, Gazala-El Alamein	36	375	10.5
1914 von Kluck	32	220	6.9
1812 Napoleon, attack on Russia	83	600	7.2
1805 Napoleon, Boulogne-Vienna	82	750	9.1
1096 Godfrey de Bouillon, First Crusade to Constantinople	127	1625	12.8

Any discussion of the relative amount of time devoted to
movement "in" and "out" of action in these operations
would necessarily be extended and very involved, so let us
simply accept the data as they stand—perhaps remembering that the armored force examples still qualify as "blitz-
kriegs" when compared to operations in World War I.
What then of the Mongols? Their messengers, traveling
from post station to post station, regularly rode from 250
to 300 miles a day. Their major units, under pressure, could
march from 80 to 100 miles a day for considerable periods
of time. According to Squadron Leader Walker,[9] in the
campaign of 1213 against the Kin Empire,

> . . . the army under Jenghiz Khan rode some eight hun-
> dred miles, stormed twenty-eight important cities and were
> repulsed from four others, in approximately one hundred
> and twenty days. If we allow a delay of two days on the
> average for the siege and capture of each city, then it means
> that the army averaged over twelve miles a day for four
> months in the depths of winter. It is true of course, that the
> Mongol armies would be split up into many detachments,
> so that the delay of one detachment need not necessarily

[9] Walker, *Squadron Leader C. C., Jenghiz Khan*, London, Luzac & Co.
1939, pp. 59-60.

mean the halting of the whole army; but nevertheless delays due to sieges must be deducted from the movement. The right wing under the three sons of Jenghiz Khan marched some three hundred miles farther, and took some thirty cities of major importance: if we make the same deductions for delays, it means that the right wing averaged about seventeen miles a day for over three months.

When we take into consideration that it was the Mongol practice to round up the natives, force them to do the hard labor of the siege, and then drive them into the breaches ahead of their own forces, two days per siege seems a low estimate. Very well, then, how fast did they move? Michael Prawdin, in *The Mongol Empire*,[10] describes their invasion of Europe in 1241:

> At the first news of the advance of the Tartars, King Bela [of Hungary] hastened to the Carpathians, had the passes blocked by abattis, called up the frontier population for military service, and entrusted the command to an experienced paladin. Then he summoned a Reichstag in Buda, and issued orders that all men fit for service should procure arms and hold themselves ready to march.
> But before the Reichstag could discuss and agree upon measures of defense, on March 10th a messenger arrived hot-foot to say that the Tartars were already attacking the passes through the Carpathians. Ere reinforcements could be sent, the paladin who had been put in command arrived with disastrous tidings. On March 12th, the Mongols had stormed the defiles, had forced surrender, had butchered the whole garrison. He himself managed to escape with a few of his men. Within a day of this, on March 15th, the first Mongolian tuman was already outside the walls of Pest, *having in three days ridden through 200 miles of hostile territory burning and slaying on the way.* [Italics mine.—R.B.]

---

10 Prawdin, *op. cit.*, p. 261.

There is much more, but let us go on to Prawdin's summing up:

> In little more than a month the entire countryside from the Baltic to the Danube had been occupied and ravaged by the Mongols: Poland, Lithuania, Silesia, and Moravia had been laid waste no less than Bukovina, Moldavia, Wallachia, and Transylvania. The towns were heaps of ruins, the land was depopulated, the armies had been dispersed, the fortresses taken by storm.

We need not go on to discuss the unbelievable rides over the deserts and mountains of all Asia, the successful winter campaigns into Russia, the 4000 mile sweep of Subutai and Chepe Noyon from Samarkand almost to Baghdad and thence by way of the Caucasus up into the Crimea and the Ukraine before turning once more toward Mongolia. The important point is that through their speed and endurance, their independence of supply, their flexibility and discipline, the Mongol armies were able to express maximum M over maximum space in minimum time over *every* phase of the military equation, and in doing so to avoid any critical realization of V. It is unfair, however, to compare them with modern armored forces to the disadvantage of the latter, for—with the single exception of Israel, and that in a restricted area and for a limited situation—no nation in our times has seriously tried to endow its forces with any comparably uniform mobility. Certainly, the armored forces of every major nation have been tied to much less mobile elements. The United States, the only country with the industrial establishment to have tried this during World War II—and perhaps even to have solved the supply problems which it would inevitably have involved—did in fact mechanize barely up to the German level, which was dictated by Germany's inferior industrial potential.

It is tempting to speculate on what might have happened had we formed, say, fifty armored divisions with their accompanying armored artillery and troop carriers, given them superior air cover, and then used a diminished and less expensive "strategic" bombing force in direct connection with deep strategic penetrations of the sort advocated by Liddell Hart, instead of wasting so much money and metal in trying to prove the correctness of Giulio Douhet's evil dream.

As matters stand, any restoration of mobility in the field would, on first examination, seem as improbable as Captain Montfort says it is. There is, however, one tantalizing possibility: the development of light nuclear or other radical agencies of vehicular power to the point where they could be practically employed in armored vehicles. This would free armored forces from their shortest leash—their dependence on a continuing fuel supply—and would also, by eliminating the internal combustion engine and its inflammable fuels, render them at once more efficient and less vulnerable. With adequate new weapons—again, perhaps made possible by such power sources—together with improved shielding and armor, adequate air filtration, and superior air cover and co-operation, forces of this sort might very well prove capable of the second-third phase radii of expression necessary to strike effectively at the armed-camp nation and its armed forces.

However, it seem that such a force at present would be more appropriate to some "third power," waiting hungrily to effect the conquest of a war-torn world, than it would be to nations which place their main reliance on today's nuclear heavy artillery, for any one of these that might attempt its use against another would almost certainly provoke the massive retaliation for which each is prepared.

T and T',
the Third Phase:
Maneuver

As has been pointed out, it is seldom possible today to draw a sharp dividing line between the second phase (Logistics) and the third (Maneuver). This is particularly true in highly developed regions, like Europe, where the existence of superior communications facilities makes rapid movement and continuous fronts possible. It is perhaps rather less so in the steppes of Central Asia, in the heart of Africa, and in other undeveloped or underdeveloped areas, but even in these, the clear-cut phase distinctions of traditional warfare are becoming obscured.

However, let us once more pretend that these changes have not taken place, and consider time in the third (Maneuver) phase as if it could still be isolated in the traditional pattern of Clausewitzian tactics—in other words, as it would apply to movement in "engagements" pure and simple.

Here, T and T' will depend partly on space, partly on the characteristics of the elements involved, and partly on the other basic values as they develop in the specific equation. The mobility of units, the separate mobility of their subunits, the rate at which they can realize potential M under the conditions given, and their vulnerability—all these, together with the corresponding factors for the enemy, must be considered. The nature of weapons is especially important, for it is a basic determinant of the character, not only of combat elements but of supporting ones, dictating at once their capabilities and limitations. Weapons, for instance, largely determine battlefield formations. Weapons like the arquebus, with a slow rate of fire and restricted range, dictate close order and several ranks, for their potential can be realized in no other way, and an enemy employing the same weapons will be too limited to exploit the resulting V concentrations to the full. These formations, again, decide the time required for deployment from march to battle order, for a change of front or a disengagement, or indeed for any of the evolutions of the battlefield.

It follows from this that a very large part of the art of generalship, in the third phase as well as in the second, has always been the ability to perceive what the enemy can and cannot do in the time available to him, and to take appropriate advantage of the situation. This is reflected in every set of rules, maxims, and principles of war. It is illustrated with singular clarity by those situations where conditions of terrain prevent the realization of normal mobility: in river-crossing battles, for example, where one side is forced to fight with the crossing not completed; in localities where natural obstacles inhibit movement; in situations where an advantage of the ground enables inferior forces to "fix" superior ones while refusing action during the time needed for a decisive localized equation to reach its point of critical imbalance. The great captain moves and strikes in such a manner that his opponent either cannot move, or else must move too late to strike effectively.

Mobility can always be a determinant of T and T', but in this phase more than in any other the degree of its realization is determined by $M\rightarrow$ and $M'\rightarrow$, $V\rightarrow$ and $V'\rightarrow$, and therefore by the T and T' values of other subordinate equations. If, for example, an action involving one flank of a battle approaches the point where its local equation becomes critically unbalanced, then the remaining time values of *that* equation will determine the realized value of mobility for any reserves and reinforcements on the way.

Again, if the vulnerability of moving elements is too high, and if adequate destructive force can be expressed against them, their potential mobility will be of purely academic interest and will not be a determinant of time in the equation as a whole.

Mobility is a determinant, not of *M per se*, but of the radius of expression of mobile elements, and therefore of the value of M which can be expressed within that radius in a given time. It cannot be too often emphasized that, while mobility in both the logistics and maneuver phases always confers an advantage, it has no military value *in itself*. In the equations of war, it is always an enabling factor—*a substitute for weapons of infinite range, accuracy, and destructive power,* and a roundabout way of accomplishing what such ideal weapons might accomplish directly. It is of value only because it implements the realization of M or prevents the realization of V by the enemy. (Parenthetically, one of the two great errors made by many of the early apostles of "air power"—and shared, unfortunately, by some of their successors today—was the premature belief that they had indeed found this ideal weapon in the long-range bomber. Their second error, which compounded and perpetuated the first, was in allowing themselves to become so fired up by Douhetian ferocity and bombast that any dispassionate assessment became impossible to them. They failed to see that the bomber, however swift, was not a new mobile element in the traditional sense, but part—and a temporary part—of the fourth phase curve of artillery development.)

To sum it up, the mobility of all elements must serve one purpose: the achievement of that *unbalanced equation* which is the only proper goal of generalship, and which I will discuss more fully in the next chapter.

T and T',
Fourth and Fifth
(Weapons) Phases

Time, in the two weapons phases, assumes an aspect rather different from its previous ones, for we can take it as axiomatic that, with two general areas of exception, the flight time of individual projectiles is not significant to the equation, and that the T factor for a single shell burst is even less likely to be so. The first area of exception involves projectiles with flight times long enough to render them vulnerable to counter-weapons of various sorts: aircraft and ICBMs, for instance. The second involves weapons of precision employed against moving targets: anti-aircraft and counter-missile missiles. In these cases, flight time can be extremely critical, an absolute determinant of success or failure.

Even in the case of much less advanced weapons, there have of course been rare exceptions to the general rule. Charles Winthrop Sawyer[11] tells of an attempt by Civil War sharpshooters to kill an enemy general with a heavy bench-rest rifle at a range of more than eighteen hundred yards, and even if the episode is apocryphal it is worth recounting. Changing wind conditions and the command timetable hastened the carefully prepared shot, and, when the general obstinately remained in his tent, the decision was made to shoot at his second-in-command, seated outside with two other officers. The shot was fired. The general left the tent. The three officers rose and saluted. The one who had been fired at moved to one side—and the general stepped forward just in time to be killed by the bullet! But such events are scarcely in the normal order of things!

---

[11] Sawyer, Charles Winthrop, *Firearms in American History*, 1920.

Ordinarily T and T′ in these phases must refer either to the time required for the expression of a given value of destructive force by a single weapon used repeatedly or by a multiplicity of weapons, or else to the time needed for the realization of a given value of vulnerability. Basically, of course, T will be determined by the nature and number of weapons employed and by the vulnerability of the agencies employing them, and this value will then be modified by strictures of terrain and situation, as well as by the other factors of the local equation and by associated relevant processes.

Time in the Equations of Limited War

In the picture of limited war today, one thing is certain: this is an age neither of classical military simplicity nor, at least for the present—with an occasional, very rare exception—of classically decisive warfare. Some mention has already been made of the vast discrepancies existing between the mobility factors not only of our more highly specialized elements, but of the individual elements themselves operating in different phases or under differing conditions of terrain. Let us consider such extreme examples as that of airborne infantry in the second (Logistics) and third (Maneuver) phases; of carrier-borne aircraft which, if their parent ship happens to be too huge to pass through the Panama Canal, cannot realize their own mobility until it has traveled half around the world at twenty-some-odd knots; of the time-consuming setting up of increasingly complex support and supply networks which must precede the employment of even the most mobile elements.

Genghis Khan, in planning his campaigns, had to consider one value of mobility and one only, at least where his own forces were concerned. The sole exception lay in the walled cities he was compelled to take, and once the Mongols had developed their siege techniques even these—as we have seen—seldom slowed him down significantly. Mobility, for the Mongols, was a single, universal constant, slightly modified by terrain and by the weather. Consequently, T was easily and almost universally predictable.

Compare this to the problems facing MacArthur in Korea or, even worse, United States commanders in Vietnam. Their armies are so heterogeneous, their ability to move so various and inconstant, that the estimation of probable T is immeasurably more complex. In either case the forces of the enemy, while simpler than their own, are still far more diverse and complex than any which the Mongols, in their day, had to face. To complicate matters even further, the fact that almost all the elements of a modern army are limited to their own specialized functions renders the calculation of probable T, both in the local and over-all equations, far more difficult than it has ever been, for nowadays inter-element substitutions and extemporizations are much less often possible, and consequently interdependence is much more absolute than it once was. This means, of course, that accurate judgment of every other potential value in the equation, of $M\rightarrow$ and $M'\rightarrow$, $V\rightarrow$ and $V'\rightarrow$, has been made not only more difficult, but therefore also less likely. For time, once more, is a dimension of every military process; if it cannot be evaluated accurately in potential, neither can the process as a whole.

The
Critical
Imbalance

In considering the equations of war, or in employing them to evaluate a situation or predict the outcome of an operation, one point must always be kept in mind: the equations of war *are not* the processes which they describe; the map *is not* the territory. This may appear absurdly obvious; however, it actually is not. Only too often, where the processes of both peace and war are concerned, the "map" in the thinker's mind becomes so thoroughly identified with the process under consideration that imperceptibly the latter is lost sight of, and we find the mental analogue of reality being regarded as though it actually *were* real. (An excellent example of this may be found in the maps of social structure and process advanced by Marxists, which fre-

CHAPTER 4

The equations of war always have two sets of values: one's own and the enemy's. When these are too nearly balanced, the attrition of force tends to be slow, and action indecisive. When, by military art or natural circumstances, they are thrown sharply out of balance, attrition can be swift and action decisive. The battles and campaigns where decisive victories are achieved are usually those in which a critical imbalance has been established—that point of no return where, inevitably, the enemy's realized vulnerability escalates and his force decays. Therefore the critical imbalance should be the goal of all military theory, of all military planning, of all commanders.

quently bear no relation to present-day realities, and, indeed, little enough to the early Nineteenth Century realities from which they purport to have been derived.) Count Alfred Korzybski, father of General Semantics, formulated these principles more than thirty-five years ago and published them in his basic work, *Science and Sanity.*[1] Their influence has been wide and varied, more often than not unacknowledged, and frequently indirect.

The equations descriptive of a process are abstractions from the reality of the process itself, and from like proc-

---

[1] Korzybski, *Count* Alfred, *Science and Sanity, an Introduction to Non-Aristotelian Systems and General Semantics,* Lancaster, Pa., Science Press Printing Co., 2d. ed., 1941

esses. It follows, therefore, that if the wrong characteristics are abstracted, or if the wrong abstractions are made from the "right" characteristics, no accurate equation can be written or imagined. Thus, an illiterate peasant sees a one-eyed crone a few hours before his donkey dies; he mentions this unusual circumstance to a friend or relative, who remembers, or thinks that he remembers, or thinks that he may have heard someone else remember seeing a similar old woman before his cow fell ill; *ergo*, such encounters either presage ill luck to livestock or, even worse, the women themselves evilly cause the happening. All very logical, and all completely divorced from reality. The example may appear extreme, but such are the perils of verbal logic, and that is why it is always necessary to maintain what Korzybski called *the consciousness of abstracting—* an awareness, not only of *what* we know or think we know, but also of the processes by which we know it and of the fact that our "knowledge" is not the exterior reality.

Militarily, the absence of such an awareness has often resulted in the adoption and persistence of dominating doctrines which are in reality little more than glorified catchphrases, and sometimes, ultimately, in the senseless loss of hundreds of thousands of good men to "prove" them. Two that come instantly to mind are Danton's *"L'audace, l'audace, toujours l'audace!"* and the concept of the *offensive à outrance*.

Because of the overriding importance of achieving the unbalanced equation in the positive aspect, and of avoiding it in the negative, before we discuss it we must make certain that we never mistake our mathematical or, more often, quasi-mathematical descriptions of military processes for the processes themselves. In actuality, it is the *process* which must be unbalanced. We cannot rest content simply because the equation descriptive of it *appears* unbalanced. We must invariably assure ourselves that the reality is accurately and adequately evaluated, and so represented in its symbolic analogue. We cannot afford the lazy luxury of stable values and unchanging definitions, for the values we must measure and the processes we must define are never completely stable or completely static.

The Nature of the Critical Imbalance

What is the unbalanced equation in war—the *decisively* unbalanced equation? Where does the military equation reach its point or area of critical imbalance? What may be done to ensure that the equation is already decisively unbalanced at the outset of a military process, or so to manipulate its factors that it will become favorably unbalanced as soon as possible? These are key questions, for all the answers to them, if they could be found, would comprehend not only the whole art of war, but the even more profound problem of where war ceases to be practicable. We can at least search for some of them in the realized and recorded equations of past wars, in the operative equations of present wars, and in the potential equations of wars in the future.

Because the past is no longer fluid, because its quantities and values are very largely known, there is the temptation to give it too much time, too much attention, analyzing dead battles and dead campaigns much as one might analyze long-finished chess games. A certain amount of this must be done, but I will try to confine it here to those few instances necessary for the exemplification of principle, for —aside from its purely intellectual interest—the military past is important to us only as its study casts light on the military future; as we have seen, because of vast and rapid changes in techniques and instruments, the past is as full of snares and delusions as it is of valid lessons. There can be no direct translation of past relationships to today's equations; in each case, the process must be expressed as pure principle, and then the principle must be applied to modern values and conditions. This is true of vulnerability, of destructive force, of time, and of the equation as a whole; it is true, therefore, of the area of critical imbalance.

Roughly speaking, this area can be defined as that stage of any military process where the ratio of $M\rightarrow$ to $M'\rightarrow$ (and it must be remembered that we are dealing here with *relevant* destructive force) starts irretrievably to escalate according to a geometrical progression, and/or (and this is functionally the same) where the realized $V'\rightarrow$ to $V\rightarrow$ relationship does likewise. This may occur in a single phase or in a complex of the phases of expression, and it can be brought about in an interesting variety of ways.

1. In perhaps its simplest form, it can occur as a consequence of the mutual attrition of two initially disparate forces, especially when circumstances forbid or ignorance prevents redressing the balance by art or stratagem. In such cases, Lanchester's N^2 Law, or something very similar, applies directly. A hundred Vikings, shall we say, attack half a hundred others in a situation where space restricts, or custom fails to provide a pattern for, effective maneuver. Then, everything else being equal, it is inevitable that any formation the weaker force assumes will be broken; its surviving members will find themselves facing not only enemies before them, but others on their flanks and to their rear. Short of Thor's unlikely intervention, there can be only one development of such an equation, one end to such a battle.

2. In those more complex situations where maneuver is forbidden neither by nature nor by doctrine, the critical imbalance can be brought about by the proper disposition and direction of available force, even when the initial imbalance may be unfavorable. Because of its beautiful simplicity and clarity, I have chosen Mr. Lanchester's analysis of Nelson's Memorandum before Trafalgar[2] to exemplify this, even though the scheme he proposed in it was not, because of the final relative strengths of the two fleets, followed exactly.

> ... The old order [Lanchester states] was to give battle in parallel columns or lines, ship to ship, the excess of ships, if either force were numerically superior, being doubled on the rear ships of the enemy. It was not until the "Battle of the Saints," in 1782, that a change took place; Rodney (by accident or intention) broke away from tradition, and cutting through the lines of the enemy, was able to concentrate on his centre and rear, thereby achieving a decisive victory.[3]

He then continues with this exposition:

> § 40. *British Naval Tactics in 1805. The Nelson "Touch."* The accident or experiment of 1782 had evidently become the established tactics of the British in the course of the twenty years which followed, for not only do we find the method in question carefully laid down in the plan of attack given in the Memorandum issued by Nelson just prior to the Battle of Trafalgar in 1805, but the French Admiral Villeneuve confidently asserted in a note issued to his staff in anticipation of the battle that:—"The British Fleet will not be formed in a line-of-battle parallel to the combined fleet according to the usage of former days. Nel-

---

[2] Lanchester, *op. cit.*

[3] It would be interesting to determine the exact extent of the influence of John Clerk of Eldin, whose *Treatise on Naval Tactics* went into several editions and was read with favor by Lord Nelson. Clerk's ideas appear to have influenced a number of important naval figures even before the action of Rodney's referred to by Lanchester.

son, assuming him to be, as represented, really in command, will seek to break our line, envelop our rear, and overpower with groups of his ships as many as he can isolate and cut off." Here we have a concise statement of a definite tactical scheme based on a clear understanding of the advantages of fire concentration.

It will be understood by those acquainted with the sailing-ship of the period that the van could only turn to come to the assistance of those in the rear at the cost of a considerable interval of time, especially if the van should happen to be to leeward of the centre and rear. The time taken to "wear ship," or in light winds to "go about" (often only to be effected by manning the boats and rowing to assist the manœuvre), was by no means an inconsiderable item. Thus it would not uncommonly be a matter of some hours before the leading ships could be brought within decisive range, and take an active part in the fray.

§ 41. *Nelson's Memorandum and Tactical Scheme.* In order further to embarrass the enemy's van, and more effectively to prevent it from coming into action, it became part of the scheme of attack that a few ships, a comparatively insignificant force, should be told off to intercept and engage as many of the leading ships as possible; in brief, to fight an independent action on a small scale; we may say admittedly a losing action. In this connection Nelson's memorandum of October 9 is illuminating. Nelson assumed for the purpose of framing his plan of attack that his own force would consist of forty sail of the line, against forty-six of the combined (French and Spanish) fleet. These numbers are considerably greater, as things turned out, than those ultimately engaged; but we are here dealing with the memorandum, and not with the actual battle. The British Fleet was to form in two main columns, comprising sixteen sail of the line each, and a smaller column of eight ships only. The plan of attack prescribed in the event of the enemy being found in line ahead was briefly as follows: —One of the main columns was to cut the enemy's line about the centre, the other to break through about twelve ships from the rear, the smaller column being ordered to engage the rear of the enemy's van three or four ships ahead of the centre, and to frustrate, as far as possible,

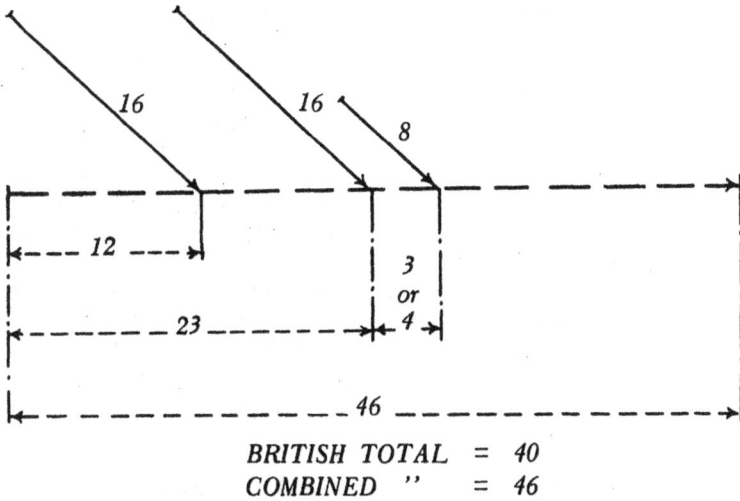

BRITISH TOTAL   =   40
COMBINED   ''   =   46

Fig. 10.

every effort the van might make to come to the succour of
the threatened centre or rear. Its object, in short, was to
prevent the van of the combined fleet from taking part in
the main action. The plan is shown diagrammatically in
Fig. 10.

§ 42. *Nelson's Tactical Scheme Analysed.* An examination of the numerical values resulting from the foregoing
disposition is instructive. The force with which Nelson
planned to envelop the half—*i.e.*, 23 ships—of the combined
fleet amounted to 32 ships in all; this according to the n^2 law
would give him a superiority of fighting strength of almost
exactly two to one,* and would mean that if subsequently
he had to meet the other half of the combined fleet, without
allowing for any injury done by the special eight-ship column, he would have been able to do so on terms of equality.
The fact that the van of the combined fleet would most
certainly be in some degree crippled by its previous encounter is an indication and measure of the positive advantage of strength provided by the tactical scheme. Dealing with the position arithmetically, we have:—

* $23 \times \sqrt{2} = 32.5$

Strength of British (in arbitrary n^2 units),

$$32^2 + 8^2 = 1088$$

And combined fleet,

$$23^2 + 23^2 = 1058$$

British advantage   30

Or, the numerical equivalent of the remains of the British Fleet (assuming the action fought to the last gasp), $= \sqrt{30}$ or $5\frac{1}{2}$ ships.

If for the purpose of comparison we suppose the total forces had engaged under the conditions described by Villeneuve as "the usage of former days," we have:—

Strength of combined fleet, 46^2 .... $= 2116$
     "   British   " 40^2 .... $= 1600$

Balance in favour of enemy   516

Or, the equivalent numerical value of the remainder of the combined fleet, assuming complete annihilation of the British, $= \sqrt{516} = 23$ ships approximately.

Thus we are led to appreciate the commanding importance of a correct tactical scheme. If in the actual battle the old-time method of attack had been adopted, it is extremely doubtful whether the superior seamanship and gunnery of the British could have averted defeat. The actual forces on the day were 27 British sail of the line against the combined fleet numbering 33, a rather less favourable ratio than assumed in the Memorandum. In the battle, as it took place, the British attacked in two columns instead of three, as laid down in the Memorandum; but the scheme of concentration followed the original idea. The fact that the wind was of the lightest was alone sufficient to determine the exclusion of the enemy's van from the action. However, as a study the Memorandum is far more important than the actual event, and in the foregoing analysis it is truly remarkable to find, firstly, the definite statement of the cutting the enemy into two *equal* parts— according to the *n-square* law the exact proportion corresponding to the reduction of his total effective strength to a minimum; and, secondly, the selection of a proportion, the nearest whole-number equivalent to the $\sqrt{2}$ ratio of theory, required to give a fighting strength equal to tackling the two halves of the enemy on level terms, and the detachment of the remainder, the column of eight sail, to weaken and impede the leading half of the enemy's fleet to guarantee the success of the main idea. If, as might fairly be assumed, the foregoing is more than a coincidence, it suggests itself that Nelson, if not actually acquainted with the *n-square* law, must have had some equivalent basis on which to figure his tactical values.

In actuality, Nelson divided his twenty-seven sail of the line into two divisions, twelve ships under his own command in the forward column and fifteen under Collingwood in the rear line. According to the latter,[4] Nelson broke through the enemy's line "about the tenth ship from the van, and the second in command about the twelfth ship from the rear," thereby splitting the allied fleet in three: ten, eleven, twelve, or thereabouts. (Accounts vary somewhat, but their variance is not too significant to the relational pattern.) It is easy enough to work out the arithmetical result according to the N^2 Law, which gives Collingwood a superiority of 196 to 144 even if we discount his slowest vessel, which did not arrive in time to take a serious part in the action. The apparent validity of that law is, however, of secondary interest. What is vastly more important here is that both the planned and the actual battle so clearly exemplify the critical imbalance. We can assume, I think, that the vulnerability of British and French and Spanish ships of the line at that time was virtually identical. We can grant the British a very decided edge in seamanship and gunnery. The rest lies in the fact that Nelson planned and achieved an action *the equation of which was critically unbalanced in his favor from the start.* While Villeneuve might conceivably have altered the margin by

[4] Thursfield, James R., *Nelson and Other Naval Studies,* New York, E. P. Dutton & C., 1920, p. 36.

which Nelson beat him, there was nothing he could have done to restore the balance or prevent the victory. As it was, the French and Spanish lost all but eleven ships, which escaped to Cadiz; the British lost none.

Another example of Nelson's ability to bring about a favorable critical imbalance where the initial measure of force actually appeared to be against him was the earlier (1798) Battle of the Nile, where with thirteen 74's and one 50-gun vessel he destroyed a French fleet of thirteen ships of the line, which outgunned him, and four frigates. The French admiral, Brueys, lay in an apparently secure anchorage, with shoal waters and the land to port and forward, expecting that whatever attack might come would be against his rear. Because of this, he had cleared for action only to starboard. Nelson, assuming correctly that the French would not hug the shoals too closely, took full advantage of this, sending five vessels inside their line. As for the rest, it is enough to quote one sentence from his subsequent letter to Lord Howe: "By attacking the enemy's van and centre, the wind blowing directly along their line, I was enabled to throw what force I pleased on a few ships."[5]

The French lost everything but two frigates and two ships of the line, which managed to escape. The British, again, lost not a vessel. In each instance, Nelson was able to realize a strikingly superior M—by taking advantage of the time factor. At Trafalgar, the ten ships of the Allied van could not possibly come about in time to affect the action; at the Nile, those of the French rear were similarly helpless. In both cases, their distance from the balance of their fleets needed to be measured, not in hundreds of yards, but in minutes and hours. The application of Lanchester's N^2 law to the earlier battle would show a mathematical imbalance

---

[5] Warner, Oliver, *A Portrait of Lord Nelson*, London, Penguin Books and Chatto & Windus, 1963, p. 161.

as striking as that exhibited at Trafalgar. Nelson, in short, with a mobility equivalent to that of his opponents, accomplished in each instance, through his superior disposition of his forces, what the Mongols accomplished regularly on land through their vastly superior mobility.

These two examples of action at sea were chosen to illustrate the point simply because it is more convenient to deal with a dozen or two or three closely equivalent units like ships of the line in the age of sail than to examine the complexities inevitable to the operation of diverse land forces over uneven terrain. On land, the "Classic" battle probably offers the simplest and clearest examples of similar developments of the unbalanced equation. All of Scipio Africanus' great battles illustrate it—Ilipa, Baecula, Zama; in each instance, his dispositions enabled such a realization of $M\rightarrow$, phase by phase, that no adequate realization of $M'\rightarrow$ could be achieved in the time available. The reader is urged to read Liddell Hart's admirable treatment of these battles and then to consider them with the military equation and the critical imbalance as a yardstick.[6]

To return momentarily to naval warfare, it is interesting to compare Trafalgar and the Nile to battles in which, for one reason or another, the critical imbalance never was achieved—Jutland, for example—and to others like Manila Bay, Santiago, and Tsushima Straits, where it was inherent in the measure of the forces involved. At Jutland, it is conceivable that either side—had a Nelson, a St. Vincent, a Howe, or a Collingwood been in command—might have achieved a favorable critical imbalance and won decisively. However, at Manila Bay and Santiago, the Spaniards never could have done so, no matter who commanded them, because their training, their vessels, and their ordnance were

---

[6] Liddell Hart, *Scipio Africanus,* previously cited.

so grossly inferior; and this is equally true of the Russians at Tsushima.

The Phases of Expression
of M and the
Critical Imbalance

The critical imbalance of a military situation will depend on the realized values of $M\to$ and $M'\to$, $V\to$ and $V'\to$, and can be achieved by manipulating these values in any one, or in more than one, of the phases of expression of M. However, it is possible to state as a general rule that an apparent critical imbalance in any or even all phases prior to the final weapons phases cannot seriously be considered in isolation. All must depend, ultimately, on the *final* phases of the expression of destructive force. The order of consideration, therefore, must be reversed:

1. The weapons phases.
2. The maneuver and weapons phases, always taken *together*.
3. The logistics, maneuver, and weapons phases, always taken together.
4. The preparatory, logistics, maneuver, and weapons phases, always taken together.

It is in the ultimate weapons phases that $M\to$ actually achieves its realization. We can grant that frequently the less tangible determinants of M and M', V and V'—doctrine and morale and training—can change realized values in the weapons phases drastically. However, as they are enabling factors, multipliers whose maximum value in any military equation is exactly 1, they must always be weighed very carefully and realistically. They cannot *substitute* for deficiencies in the "earlier" phases which provide the physical weapons they impel; nor can they, if they are themselves inadequate, bring those potential values to full realization. (This subject is important and interesting enough to merit more detailed consideration, which it will presently receive, for in no area of military judgment and planning have there been such great and tragic errors as in the estimation of these intangible determinants.)

A high potential M and low V measured against a low potential M′ and high V′ in *any* of the phases of expression can result in a serious critical imbalance. However, it cannot be repeated too often that this imbalance must be real rather than illusory; it must apply to the entire equation concerned, whether this be for a skirmish, a battle, a campaign, or a war. It is easy enough to define a true critical imbalance in dealing with a single action on sea or land, but it is much more difficult to do so where a complexity of operations is involved. The touchstone is, first, the ultimate effect—if any—on the weapons phases in specific operations separately considered, and secondly, the effect of these operations on the grand equation of the "campaign" or the "war." Here we hark back to Clausewitz's definitions of tactics and strategy, but from a very different viewpoint and, I think, in terms more universally and accurately applicable.

If we recall the processes involved in the expression of destructive force, it immediately becomes obvious that a prime purpose of M is always to inhibit these processes in any or all the phases to prevent the ultimate realization of M′. It is precisely here, however, that an accurate judgment of realities is essential. To refer once again to Clausewitz, an "engagement" won, no matter how decisively, can be of no great military significance *unless it substantially influences the outcome of more important operations.* Inhibitory actions, in any phase, can have no true significance in their local context only; that must invariably lie in their ultimate effect. Thus, the destruction of a factory by "strategic bombardment" is significant only if, directly or indirectly, it affects the weapons phases of the expression of M, and does so *in time*. If communications are to be cut, if movement and maintenance are to be interrupted, the same rule applies. For instance, anyone placing troops athwart Genghis Khan's supply lines would indeed have been engaging in a futile exercise, for he was in no way dependent on them.

Of course, the history of war is filled with tales of heroic, dramatic, emotionally memorable, sometimes "victorious," *and utterly indecisive and ineffectual* actions. Two very simple instances are Cardigan's charge at Balaklava and Sitting Bull's expert manhandling of the 7th Cavalry at the Little Big Horn. Whatever the former did for literature, it accomplished nothing militarily. The latter at least had the merit of being "successful," but, regardless of its eventual influence on innumerable nauseating TV scripts, it had no effect whatever on the inescapable destiny of the Plains Indians.

Even these episodes have provoked endless wranglings, apologies, accusations. To what end? Failure, for whatever reason, is failure still, whether it be Custer's in the field or his opponent's on the plains of history. Germany failed to win the First World War; the Allies finally won it only by erosion. In World War II, Germany did succeed in creating a critical imbalance which brought about the fall of France, but again she failed to win the war itself. There is no shortage of military blundering or of military failures in one degree or another. To avoid them in the future, it is necessary to examine those which have occurred—but only for their whys and wherefores. It is senseless to scream *Nous sommes trahis!*—however learnedly—or to engage in any fishwives' game of vituperation. We should concern ourselves with failure only so that we can understand its causes in terms of military theory; if personalities or politics become involved, we can accept the fact, but we should waste no time on it. The study of success—and especially of those successes which follow on the achievement of a critical imbalance on the grand scale—is far more valuable. Leaders who understand the real reasons for successes of this order cannot fail to understand also the causes of failure, for the second must inevitably follow from the first.

The Critical Imbalance in the Maneuver and Logistics Phases

In these phases, everything else being equal, an unbalanced equation—and conceivably a critical imbalance—can be achieved by any one or combination of four factors:

1. *Superior "mobility," positive:* the ability to concentrate or deploy M values faster than the enemy can concentrate or deploy values of M'.
2. *Superior "mobility," negative:* the ability to reduce V values by withdrawing or dispersing V units, or by taking advantage of terrain features, faster than the enemy can similarly reduce V' values.
3. *Superior judgment:* lacking superior mobility, the ability so to dispose one's forces, in a given situation or under conditions deliberately selected, that the enemy's equal or even superior mobility is negated.
4. *Effective inhibition:* weapons phase operations designed specifically to prevent the enemy from realizing 1 and/ or 2 above.

This grouping together of the maneuver and logistics phases may seem strange. However, as we have seen, in modern war the two almost invariably overlap and merge —as, indeed, do all the phases except the preparatory. Besides, in principle there is no difference between the "mobility" of weapons and that of men, munitions, or miscellaneous materiel. Nor is mobility merely a matter of rate of movement. If Army A and Army B have the same rate of movement over roads, and if, to reach a given critical position, Army A has only one road available while its opponent has three of equivalent capacity, then its *functional* mobility in these phases—its ability to realize M values at a certain place and time—will be a fraction of the enemy's. By the same token, if supplies on which an army is dependent travel more slowly than the army does itself, then every hour lost is lost not only by the mechanisms of supply but to the army as a whole—immediately if the dependency is immediate, ultimately if the dependence is less direct. Time and energy are to some extent convertible in the equation: a man or a truck or any other element that takes four days to do a job which could be done in two is subtracting two days *and an equivalent amount of work from* its own military potential and from the army's. In either the maneuver or logistics phase, therefore, any inhibition of the enemy's activity towards the realization of M' is worthwhile if it can be accomplished at low enough cost, provided only that the force employed for the purpose is not thereby diverted from more important tasks. A main concern of the commander must always be to plan such operations not just to harass the enemy and sap his strength, but with a view toward the creation of a critical imbalance. To be fully effective, these operations must be directed against enemy efforts on which M, in its ultimate phases, is directly dependent.

We have seen how, repeatedly, the Mongols were able to create a critical imbalance through mobility. We have seen how Nelson accomplished the same end through superior judgment and superior dispositions.

Our own World War II campaigns in the Pacific present

superb examples of the employment of both methods in order to achieve a critical imbalance not only in individual actions, but in the grand equation of the war against Japan. Like traditional war on land, war over the vast spaces of the sea offers a picture of relatively small forces operating over great distances; when such a war becomes an amphibious war of positions, the similarity becomes even stronger. Every phase in the expression of M→ becomes clear in such a war; one can again distinguish battle from campaign; Clausewitz's definition of tactics and strategy appears to regain its meaning. Sea-air superiorities are made available, and an effective war is waged against sources of Japan's strength and against the communications on which her scattered armies in the Pacific and part of mainland Asia must depend. These sea-air superiorities are employed to win naval victories more clearly decisive than any in modern warfare (or at least any fought against a skillful, resolute, and well-armed enemy). They are employed to enable superior land forces to overwhelm certain key Japanese positions, effectively isolating and neutralizing others, and making possible the great offensives into the Philippines and—had there been no surrender—against Japan itself.

Parenthetically, I remember how obvious it was, while all this was going on, that the turning point had come, that a true critical imbalance had indeed been achieved, that neither a Nogi nor a Togo—could one have been found among Japan's boastful, self-admiring generals and [perhaps less culpable] admirals—that neither such a leader nor the undiminished courage of his soldiery could have averted total defeat and utter ruin. This fact, by the way, is too frequently obscured by the dramatic and horrifying impact of Hiroshima and Nagasaki. Yet for some months before the ultimate surrender—indeed from the time of Tojo's resignation—it was clear that the Japanese establishment was preparing to capitulate; and had it not been for the formula of "unconditional surrender" and for our eagerness to please the Russians—who had never been our allies against Japan—that capitulation might have been negotiated much more to our advantage. For the Japanese feared nothing so much as a Communist takeover, knowing that the Communists would have destroyed the Imperial House as ruthlessly as they destroyed the House of Romanov, and that they would have set up a new Establishment which would never have permitted its predecessor to survive. It is well to remember that Japan had bowed to superior force before, when she was opened to the world by Perry, and that she had then submitted to occupation by alien troops under treaties of extraterritoriality; and it is significant that the Emperor Hirohito, in his surrender speech, used almost the same terms as did his grandfather, the Meiji Tenno, when he told his subjects that, while foreign garrisons remained, they "must endure the unendurable."

The surface-air-subsurface-land warfare in the Pacific was a far cry from naval and amphibious warfare in Nelson's day, but, compared to any major modern war on a continental land mass, it retained much of the old simplicity. Discrete actions were not lost in the confusing picture of vast and seemingly amorphous land operations; great successes and great errors alike stood out quite clearly because of the clear definition of their purpose. There can be no real argument about what was or was not accomplished by such victories as Midway, the Philippines Sea, or Leyte Gulf; and if, in each instance, the critical imbalance achieved may not have followed so directly on a detailed plan of action as it did at the Nile or Trafalgar, this illustrates the greatly increased complexity of the sea-air battle and in no way minimizes its decisiveness. If, again, the obvious superiority of American training, equipment, and technique played a major role in the decisions, this does not minimize the skill with which American strength was handled on all levels and in each of the phases of expression. (There will be more to say about this later when we discuss the preparatory phase and its relation to the critical imbalance.) It must be remembered that naval aircraft had *in effect* extended the gunnery radius of expression in the first phase by several hundred miles; that land-based aircraft had similarly extended the radius of expression of "shore batteries"; that the speed of surface vessels and of submarines had given them a far greater radius and independence in the maneuver and logistics phases; and, finally, that the task of considering and co-ordinating all these elements had become so complex that it was only rendered possible by advances in communications technology. Under such circumstances, genius must lie very largely in the ability first to exploit the preparatory phase to the maximum, and secondly to effect the realization of M through and during the logistics and maneuver phases while preventing any comparable realization of V by the enemy. This became pretty much standard procedure in the Pacific, and as a consequence the continuity necessary to the exploitation of a major critical imbalance was maintained throughout.

A word must be said here about this essential factor of continuity. The history of war is full of "decisive" victories which have won nothing, of campaigns won and lost again, all because continuity of expression had been allowed to lapse and an enemy already beaten permitted to revive, rebuild his strength, and renew his efforts.

One of the best examples in all history of maintained continuity—as well as of a critical imbalance accurately planned *through every phase*—appears in the six-day Israeli-Arab War of 1967. In the preparatory phase, the Israeli command had created its armed forces, composed very largely of reservists and totaling more than ten percent of the country's population; deriving their concepts very largely from the ideas of Sir Basil Liddell Hart, they had evolved a doctrine beautifully suited to the desert war confronting them; they had trained to an extremely high peak of competence and morale. The Israeli Army, unlike any other army since the time of the Mongols, appears to have been almost fully mobile *as an army*—at least within its probable radius of expression—with its armored and semi-armored units, motorized infantry and artillery, *and supply* (or at least immediate supply) moving at virtually the same rate of speed. Referring back to Captain Montfort's article, quoted in the last chapter, we find that the Israeli moved roughly four or five times as fast as did the Germans in their blitzkrieg against France, and nearly three times as fast as Rommel during his 1942 advance from Gazala to El Alamein. From the start, when Israeli aircraft created the initial critical imbalance by destroying the greater part of the Egyptian air force on the ground, until the final shattering of the Egyptian and Jordanian armies three or four days later, the pressure was unrelenting. Everywhere, and through each phase, the Israeli force expressed was *relevant* force; M was realized to its maximum, as was the vulnerability of the Arabs, V'. Meanwhile, M' was never permitted to achieve serious realization; nor was Israeli vulnerability, or V.

The objection may be raised that the numerical superiority of the Arabs in men and materiel was so far offset by their inferiority in the martial virtues and talents that any resolute opponent could have made mincemeat of them, but this objection is scarcely valid, for other Arabs, not too many years ago, were able to fight well enough to compel the French withdrawal from Algeria, and certainly the members of King Hussein's Arab Legion were anything but contemptible. A far more important factor was the Israeli understanding of the art of war.

One interesting feature of the war, incidentally, was the fact that, from the Israeli standpoint, the logistics phase can scarcely be said to have existed. The size of the country and the direct presence of Arab armies on her borders caused the preparatory phase to merge immediately, or almost immediately, into the maneuver phase. Here, once again, though for very different reasons than on the Western Front in World War I, the two words "campaign" and "battle" hardly apply with any accuracy, for by the standards of traditional war each has assumed certain characteristics of the other and any precise line of demarcation between them is hard to establish.

A little earlier, mention was made of the doctrinal debt owed by the Israelis to Sir Basil Liddell Hart—a debt which has been explicitly acknowledged by virtually every major Israeli commander. Not only is this one of the few instances where a military prophet has received the honor due him in his own time, but it leads us to another view of the critical imbalance. The Israeli generals invariably placed special emphasis on Sir Basil's "strategy of the indirect approach." This general doctrine was published originally in 1929, and again, greatly augmented and revised, in 1941. Two further editions, revised and enlarged, appeared in 1945 and 1954,[7] and it is still in print today. I know of no work which casts a clearer light on the achievement—and non-achievement—of the critical imbalance, not only by "Classical" armies and by the Mongols, but in major operations conducted by large land forces in more or less modern times—an area of enquiry which, intentionally, has not been brought within the scope of this book.

----

[7] Liddell Hart, Sir Basil, *Strategy—The Indirect Approach*, London, Faber, 1954.

The Critical
Imbalance and the
Preparatory Phase

The more "remote" a phase is from the weapons phases of expression, the more urgent it becomes to bear those final phases constantly in mind; therefore in the preparatory phase, especially in time of peace, this can be crucially important. For it is in the weapons' phases that factors contributing to an unfavorable critical imbalance can develop unnoticed.

It is senseless to equip, arm, and train elements which have little or no chance of achieving or contributing to weapons phase realization, either because of their inadequacy in one or more of the determinants of M or because of their vulnerability. It is senseless, in short, to waste time and resources on the preparation of anything but *relevant* force. Elements irrelevant to the situational probabilities are, at the best, expensively wasteful; at the worst, they invite an unfavorable critical imbalance and disaster. Thus, using a rather mild example, the time spent training the regiments of horse cavalry which the United States brought up to war strength in 1940 and 1941 was largely wasted—at least the time devoted to horsemanship and horsemastership, to cavalry close-order drill, and to the various training manual aspects of the employment of cavalry was time thrown away at considerable cost to the country. It was by no means as costly, nor was its effect as disastrous, as the price in time and money and men paid by Poland for the fine and futile cavalry she lost so quickly to German aircraft and German armor—but, had the positions of the nations been reversed, conceivably it might have been.

There is no shortage of historical examples of this sort of thing: of costly obsolescence blindly persisted in; of tactics and techniques effective in a given milieu mechanically applied to quite a different one where they are worse than useless; of contemporary relationships between the technologically determined values of M and the intrinsic value of V either ignored or officially denied; of yesterday's estimates—or, even worse, someone's recollection of yesterday's estimates—used as a basis for today's preparations for tomorrow's battles.

We have already pointed out that, while the preparatory phase *must* precede the logistics phase, and (at least with traditional instruments) the logistics phase must precede the maneuver and weapons phases, the sequence is a simple one only until operations have begun. After the initial moves are made and the first blows struck, in the majority of wars the phases occur, so far as time is concerned, in parallel. They are sequential only insofar as their end product, the direct expression of force in the weapons phases, is concerned; and each such expression of force can, in principle, be traced back down its own sequence, even if in some instances the logistics and/or maneuver phases may be skipped completely—as in the case of ICBMs. The central question, therefore, with regard to the preparatory phase especially—a question which cannot be asked too often or too pointedly—is whether an expenditure of energy in the phase *can and will result in a worth-while expression of relevant force in the weapons phases*, directly or indirectly, and in time to affect favorably the balance, and preferably the critical balance, of at least a subsidiary equation. (In our scientific age, when the power and scope of weapons are escalating constantly, this question becomes of dominant importance, and it will be discussed at greater length when we come to examine the critical imbalance in relation to the determinants of M.)

The preparatory phase actually divides into two separate stages, with rather different characteristics: the prewar stage, and the wartime stage. (This, to a lesser degree, is also true of the logistics phase, and, if we do not try to define too narrowly, perhaps sometimes the maneuver phase as well.) Thus, the first stage of the preparatory phase ended for Japan when Admiral Nagumo sailed for Hawaii; the logistics phase ended for Admiral Nagumo when his aircraft left their carriers to attack Pearl Harbor. As we have seen, Japan's first-stage preparation was based on two estimates, one reasonably accurate—the measure of our lack of preparation in the first stage; the other wholly inaccurate —a gross underestimation of our second-stage capabilities. While, at Pearl Harbor, the Japanese did indeed achieve the local critical imbalance and the success they were after, it was a success over a fleet alone and in no way hindered or threatened the sources from which that fleet would be replaced and multiplied. While the successful sneak attack did enable Japan to establish her positions in the South Pacific, neither it nor her wartime preparatory phase (second stage) capabilities were adequate to the task of achieving an over-all critical imbalance, nor to the equally important one of preventing the United States from achieving one.

The groundwork for any grand critical imbalance must be laid in the first stage of the preparatory phase, except in those instances where the weakness or miscalculation of an enemy permits second-stage resources to function fully. Hitler so miscalculated in the Battle of Britain, in his invasion of Russia, and in his underestimation of United States strength. Napoleon miscalculated differently in 1812; once he was deeply into Russia, beset by winter, unable to bring his enemy to battle, surrounded by a deliberately denuded countryside, all the resources of France and her allies ceased to exist for him; the second stage of the preparatory phase never began for the Grand Army. It is only rarely, however, that one can count on the folly or weakness of an enemy, and it is always folly on one's own part to rely on it. Therefore, prewar preparatory phase activity should be planned with the maximum potential of the probable enemy in mind; it should produce M and V values which, compared to M' and V', promise a high probability of achieving a critical imbalance in subsidiary equations; if possible, that imbalance should be achieved with a minimum of reliance of wartime (second-stage) preparatory phase activity; and, in any case, this second-stage activity should be so planned that, regardless of enemy countermeasures, it will provide the continuity of M→ necessary to the achievement of the grand critical imbalance.

Throughout both stages of the preparatory phase, then, the nation and its civil and military authorities must concentrate on selecting the optimum instruments for the expression of relevant force, on providing these instruments, and on developing the other determinants of M→ to the maximum of their potential. This must be done with a full awareness of V, intrinsic and situational. It must be done, not merely with the idea of eventually going to war, but with the definite aim of effecting a grand critical imbalance as speedily and inexpensively as possible.

No war where such an imbalance cannot be achieved should be fought—unless, like World War II, it is literally and unavoidably forced upon one. Had the United States and our allies understood these principles in the years prior to the war—had our first-stage preparatory phase activity been based realistically on the potentialities of our most probable enemies—we might not have had to fight the war at all; in any case, it would not have taken us four years to defeat what were, by comparison, *two second-rate industrial powers*. This fact has been obscured by postwar inter-allied wrangling about who was the real victor, as well as by the popular self-congratulation and hero worship which are among the many perils of victory.

The Critical
Imbalance and the
Determinants of M

Chapter 2 listed the physical determinants of M as:

1. *Weapons*, the means for expressing destructive force.
2. *Instrumentalities*, the agencies which enable that expression.
3. *Relevance*, of weapons and instrumentalities.
4. *Space*, over which force is expressed in its several phases.
5. *Time*, during which destructive force is expressed in these several phases.
6. *Maintenance*, which enables the continued expression of destructive force.

It then went on very briefly to discuss the non-physical determinants: 1. *Morale*, and 2. *Training*, to which must be added a third, *Intellect*, which of course is implicit. However, it is best left separate from the others; to a very great extent, its exercise is what this book, or indeed any other book on the theory of war, is about.

Just as the unbalanced equation is simply a special case of the equations of war generally, so is the critical imbalance simply a special case of the unbalanced equation—even though it is the special case always to be striven for or against. What we have already seen of the relationship of the physical determinants of $M\rightarrow$ to the general equation applies directly to any of its special cases. The same principles hold true. Consequently, the physical determinants in this context are discussed only briefly.

There are three basic ways in which the physical determinants can be employed to achieve a critical imbalance:

1. By *quantitative superiority*—"mass," "concentration," or whatever other synonym is used.
2. By *qualitative superiority*—of accuracy, radius of expression, etc.
3. By *technological surprise*—which itself is a special case of 2 and/or 1.

In our day, the third is of particular interest and importance, partly because of the accelerating curve of scientific progress, which promises tomorrow technological surprises undreamed of yesterday, and partly because our age is notable for its almost unbelievable failure to exploit them fully. The nature of the technological surprise, of the scientific method, and of modern industry dictate two rigid rules for its employment. The first is that *any relevant and effective technological surprise must be employed in adequate "mass" and at the proper time and place*—in other words, it must be used to produce a major critical imbalance, or, if employed to achieve minor critical imbalances, enough of these must be planned to contribute to the achievement of a major one. The second rule is that *any critical imbalance achieved by technological surprise must be effectively maintained to prevent the enemy from compensating for it.*

One does not have to look far afield to find glaring examples of the failure to understand and to observe these rules. The first German use of gas in World War I is a case in point; a potential critical imbalance was achieved, but not exploited. This was true also of the initial British employment of the tank during the same war. Where chemical agents were concerned, the Allies compensated for the German advantage speedily enough so that the first opportunities did not come again. In the case of the tank, the opportunity remained but was never seized, even at Cambrai. However, to the author's mind at least, the most deplorable and tragic instance of them all was the failure of the United States to use its post-World War II nuclear monopoly together with its vast armies, while that monopoly existed and before those armies had been hurried back to Mom's apron strings, to establish a viable and vigorous world organization and to dictate a stable peace for the world.

There have, of course, been instances of the successful employment of the technological surprise, where it did indeed either achieve a favorable critical imbalance or else —and this can be equally important—prevent the achievement of an unfavorable one. Radar, as it was used in the Battle of Britain and, later on, in the Pacific, was one of these. However, the examples of failure are far more numerous than those of startling success, partly because too many leaders have been bogged down in their own obsolescence, partly because a narrow political and financial pragmatism often exercises too much influence in the councils of war and peace, and partly because so very few people— and so very few scientists—understand how the scientific method functions in the affairs of men and what its influence on war will be.

Technological surprises, whether they be actual weapons, "delivery systems," or production methods—and please bear in mind that I am *not* talking about new and better helmets, new and more horrible systems of thuggee for "special forces," or any other militarily unimportant innovations, but of surprises like the tank when first invented, the first practical submarines (had they been sensibly exploited), the mass production of small carriers in the Tojo

War, and the atomic bomb—these technological surprises
are of full value *only when they are used.* The longer they
remain unused, the smaller becomes their value and the
chance of their ultimate realization, regardless of the
tightness of "security."

There is no need, here, to elaborate further on the role
of the physical determinants of M and M′ in achieving or
preventing a critical imbalance. Obviously, each of them
plays a part in the process, and obviously their accurate
evaluation can pose problems of great complexity. However, as these questions are discussed off and on throughout the book, let us now further consider the role of *the
non-physical determinants.*

Because, as pointed out earlier, rather than multiplying
physical force, these non-physical determinants simply
enable the maximum realization of its inherent potential,
it may have seemed to some readers that their importance
was being underestimated. This is not the case. If the value
of these determinants is zero, then, no matter how high its
potential, destructive force is as nothing; M literally cannot
exist. Similarly, in such a situation, V will be realized to an
undesirable maximum—witness the plight of the Egyptians,
fleeing shoeless and defenseless before the Israeli Army
over the sands of Sinai. Therefore, there can be no exagger-
ating the *real* importance of these determinants. They are
extremely sensitive elements of the equation—easy to mis-
understand, easy to evaluate wrongly. *Morale* and *training,*
as symbols for them, are gross (though convenient) oversimplifications, for they include factors of infinite complexity and subtlety: culture and belief, individual and
group psychology, communication and personal relationships, education and intellectual ability. What difference
is there between an Israeli tank officer with five years of
armored service and his Egyptian counterpart? How does
that Egyptian differ from his Russian opposite number,

who perhaps trained him? Why will one man fight to the death knowing his weapons are inferior or that he is hopelessly outnumbered, while another—who may be superbly equipped—will throw down his arms and surrender or run away?

Clearly, factors of such subtlety and sensitivity can often exercise a crucial influence on the balance of the equation, and can indeed produce—either by intention or by chance— a critical imbalance. They also, because of the extreme ease with which they can be wrongly valued, can prevent the achievement of such an imbalance, when all "logical" argument seems to indicate that they will be the major factors in its attainment.

Generally speaking, there are six non-physical determinants of $M\rightarrow$ and $M'\rightarrow$ in the military equation:

1. The intellectual ability to adduce an accurate "map" of contemporary military processes.
2. The intellectual ability to devise instruments and instrumentalities relevant to that "map."
3. The intellectual ability to formulate a doctrine or doctrines relevant to both map and means.
4. The intellectual ability to employ them on all relevant military levels.
5. The intellectual ability *and the moral courage* to evaluate all the determinants of M and M', V and V' realistically, without self-deception.
6. The will to fight.

At first glance, this list may appear not to include "psychological weapons" and those physical weapons which are used largely for their psychological effect. Actually, however, such weapons are comprehended within the second determinant. *Psychological weapons* can be defined as any military instrumentalities or instruments, physical or nonphysical, employed primarily for their effect on any or all of the non-physical determinants of M'. Thus, propaganda

—a non-physical instrument—can be employed either as a stimulant to enable an optimum expression of M, or as a weapon to prevent such an expression of M'. Again, an air strike against a shaken enemy can be far more important for its indirect effect on M' than for any direct physical effect it may achieve. It is axiomatic that, while the use of psychological weapons can cause an enemy to increase the realized value of his own vulnerability, it cannot possibly lower the value of one's own except indirectly by its effect on M'.

In their negative aspect—when one or more of them are seriously lacking—the non-physical determinants can also be determinants of V or V'. Thus, any major deficiency in the ability to formulate an adequate military doctrine (see 3 above) can result directly in extremely high values of realized vulnerability, such as those which characterized infantry tactics in World War I. Again, any inability, for whatever reason, to evaluate all the determinants of the equation accurately (see 5 above) can result in similarly realized V values—like those which, in naval warfare, followed the initial failure to estimate correctly the potential effectiveness of submarines. In the main, however, the negative influence of the non-physical determinants is more often indirect—that is, through the effect of their inadequacy on the values of destructive force, and hence on the realized vulnerability of one combatant or the other.

Here we enter an area of relation and interrelation so involved that we find the semantic resources of our language scarcely adequate to handle it. Military weakness and military vulnerability are not *necessarily* always synonymous, and an inordinately high value of V does not necessarily follow on a deficiency of M; too many other factors can intervene.

Therefore, in considering the equations of war, it is *always* necessary to give priority of consideration to their physical values—always remembering the enabling role of the non-physical determinants, and the rule which sets their maximum value in any military equation at precisely 1. For it cannot be repeated too often or too forcefully that the non-physical determinants are of importance *only* as they influence the realization of the physical values of the equation.

Thus, "surprise" is of importance only as it enables the realization of optimum M and V′ or prevents the realization of optimum M′ and V. This is true also of "morale." It is true of propaganda, whether used as a stimulant or as a weapon. It is true of training. It is true of staff work. It is true even of military genius. Any or all of these non-physical determinants can contribute to the critical imbalance.

But none of them—no matter how perfected—can substitute *reliably* for the essential physical components of M→. The fact that history records many instances where, to all appearances, they have been so substituted—in many of which a critical imbalance has been spectacularly achieved—does not prove otherwise, for the majority of these have been achieved against an enemy either craven, foolish, or deluded, or indeed all three. And of the deadly sins of generalship, the worst is that of assuming—until it has been proven in a contemporary context and beyond a doubt—that the enemy is any one of these.

The military response to any challenge, any problem, must be relevant and functional; and in no area have we seen so many tragically non-functional responses as in that of the non-physical determinants, in both their positive and negative aspects. In either, their incorrect evaluation can be crucial. It is hoped that the examples offered below are so clear as to be indisputable. To the first, and salient one, a separate heading is given.

**"Air Power"
and the Will
of the Enemy**

Whether or not General Giulio Douhet really influenced world air-force policy to any major degree is perhaps debatable. However, in *The Command of the Air*,[8] published in 1921 under the auspices of the Italian Ministry of War, Douhet did set forth the doctrine, if we must call it that, of the "strategic bombardment" of civilian centers for the purpose of shattering morale, and therefore we can permit him to typify the sort of thinking that culminated in Coventry and Rotterdam, Hamburg and Dresden and Tokyo. Douhet's jewel was bedded in a setting of tooth-gnashing ferocity which, read today, calls to mind all the bad taste of the Mussolini boys gloating over the Ethiopian War. A little later we shall examine some of its errors where the non-physical determinants of M and V are concerned.

For the moment, we can devote ourselves to a Douhetian pronunciamento concerning the effect of what would then have been considered massive bombardment of civilian morale.

> In the days when a nation could shield itself behind the stout armor of an army and navy, [wrote Douhet] blows from the enemy were barely felt by the nation itself, sometimes not at all. The blows were taken by institutions such as the army and navy, well organized and disciplined, materially and morally able to resist, and able to act or counteract. The air arm, on the contrary, will strike against entities less well-organized and disciplined, less able to resist, and helpless to act or counteract. It is fated, therefore,

---

[8] Douhet, Giulio, *The Command of the Air*, New York, Coward-McCann Inc., 1942, p. 188.

that the moral collapse will come about more quickly and easily. A body of troops will stand fast under intensive bombings, even after losing half or two-thirds of its men; but the workers in shop, factory, or harbor will melt away after the first losses.

It is difficult to explain how Douhet could have been unaware of all those centuries when the dividing line between soldier and civilian, combatant and non-combatant, was not as sharp as it became after the Industrial Revolution, or his apparent ignorance of such dramatic cases of civilian involvement as the Thirty Years War. Possibly his opinion derived from nothing more profound than the fact that it is necessary for people of a certain stamp to believe that other people can be terrorized into obedience, into surrender, or into panic-stricken flight.

Whatever the cause, it scarcely explains the persistence in this error of so many of his adherents everywhere, despite the clear evidence of the past thirty years, during which the error has been exposed again and again. Just as there are medaled regulars here and there who lack courage and tenacity, so are there civilians whose morale can be shattered by a bomb or two—but these are not the peoples of proud and warlike nations. As a matter of record, no important civilian populace has yet been successfully terrorized by terror bombing: neither the British nor the Germans, neither the Russians nor the Japanese. It has, in every instance, done more to stiffen morale than to break it down. In every instance, as a means towards achieving the critical imbalance—or, indeed, even towards the general unbalancing of the equation—it has proved a failure. It has wasted a vast potential which could have been used far more decisively against those military objectives in all the phases of expression on which the value of $M'\rightarrow$ and the balance of the equation were directly dependent.

Considering all this, together with rather impressive evidence that even the physical effects of mass bombardment have more often than not been inconclusive, it is strange that the great Douhetian fallacy should retain its hold on the minds of so many men who should be able to see through it. (The *terror* of nuclear bombardment is a special case. So is the *effect* of nuclear bombardment. They are of a quite different order, and demand separate consideration.)

The Non-Physical Determinants and the Critical Imbalance

The Douhetian delusion has been singled out for special treatment because, of all military fantasies, it seems to be the most difficult to exorcise, and is still very much—and very expensively—with us. Certainly, much indecisive bombardment can be justified militarily only if one believes in Douhet's theories *as revealed truth*. But the phrase "air power" seems to have had a hypnotic influence, perhaps because of the romance always associated with man's dream of flight, perhaps even more because of our deep-rooted drive to rise above a lowly enemy and hit him from on high without being hit. It is this last, I think, which consciously or subconsciously leads to such simplistic solutions as "bombing across the Yalu," an expedient which might have worked little better before the Chinese swarmed across that stream than bombing them and their supply lines did later on.

The example of Douhet's misjudgment illustrates one (or possibly two) of the four ways in which a *false* estimate of the non-physical determinants of M and M' can unbalance the equation and, sometimes, result in a critical imbalance. These are:

1. By underestimating the intellectual capacity of the enemy.
2. By underestimating the enemy's will or ability to fight, to express destructive force.
3. By overestimating one's own capabilities in either area.
4. By believing—and perhaps this is the most treacherous of them all—that gross deficiencies in the physical determinants can invariably be overcome by superior training and pumped up morale.

Actually, aside from the "air power" example, it is category 4 above which, because of the escalation of the values of physical force, is of the greatest contemporary interest.

Just over twenty-five years ago, the Japanese were boasting to themselves and to the world that their "spiritual strength," their courage and determination and faith in their Imperial destiny, could more than compensate for any superior forces that we and our allies might throw into the field. Ten years before that, Japan's military extremists were busily assassinating not only moderate civilian leaders, but also those of their fellow officers who sensibly opposed a plan for conquest which their nation was not really equipped to carry out. A decade earlier, that faction in Japan's army which favored sword and bayonet as valid weapons was prevailing over that which, more practically, believed them to be largely obsolete.

Ten years earlier still, before the first World War, even in the West advocates of the *arme blanche* were holding out against the terrible testimony of firepower.

Always the argument was much the same: *élan* would triumph; the frightened enemy would flee before cold steel; superior discipline, superior resolution, the shock of charging cavalry—these would negate rapidity and accuracy of fire. Even though the Franco-Prussian War had shown incontrovertibly that cavalry charges were no longer practical,[9] the idea that the spirit of the charge would somehow keep the charge alive refused to die. Anyone doubting this has only to read our own *Cavalry Journal* during the Second War, when in its pages one could find nostalgic articles digested from the Russian—because the Russians, technologically and industrially unable to mechanize to our own level, still had a lot of cavalry, and were, by some of these accounts at least, heroically charging everything in sight.

The Non-Functional Response

If one hopes to fight economically and decisively, if one takes the concept of the critical imbalance as a criterion and a goal, then one's response to any serious military challenge or military problem must be functional. The military means selected and employed *must* be relevant to the contemporary values of the military equation. Any non-functional response is an invitation, if not to disaster, then to protracted, indecisive and wasteful warfare.

Today, though we still stick a bayonet on the end of almost anything that shoots, the *arme blanche* as a major weapon and shock tactics by vulnerable elements against heavy fire have few advocates.

Instead, another great illusion has started to possess us— that of a new ruthlessness, almost a new savagery, and its

---

[9] Fuller, *Major General* J. F. C., *The Conduct of War, 1789-1961*, London, Eyre & Spottiswoode, 1961, pp. 120-121.

effectiveness in war. In recent centuries, it has been characteristic of civilized Western man that (with some exceptions) he has placed his main reliance on organization, training, weaponry, and the restrained and disciplined use of force. By contrast, many non-Western civilizations and primitive cultures have habitually relied on cruelty in war and barbarity against defeated enemies, partly because it was in their nature to enjoy it, and partly because they believed terror to be an effective military instrument. Such methods are not always signs of fear and weakness in their users—the Mongols, who were neither weak nor fearful, used them constantly—but they so often are that fear and weakness must always be suspected when these methods are used.

Let us consider a few examples. There seems to be little doubt that, both in Algeria and in Indochina, the armed forces of the French pretty much went native where it came to the condoned use of terror and torture. As the world has seen, it did them little good. Again, we hear too often of our own people in Vietnam turning their backs on this sort of thing when practiced there by our indigenous allies.

Terror is one aspect. Another is the tendency to try to compensate for inadequacies in doctrine or technology by intensifying training in obsolete or obsolescent weapons and techniques, or in weapons and techniques of greatly restricted usefulness, provided that they are dramatic enough.

The psychological background for the first method, (the use of terror), can be traced, through today's pervading atmosphere of violence, at least to Germany's open espousal of *schrechtlichkeit*,[10] during the Kaiser War, and

---

[10] Morgan *Brigadier General* J. H., *Assize of Arms* . . . , New York, Oxford University Press, 1946.

perhaps to the naive military pragmatism and fury of the French Revolution. The second, though not entirely unrelated, probably has a more immediate origin in the formation of the so-called commandos when Britain, fighting alone and fighting for her life, was unable to strike any major blows across the Channel except by air. Their successes, though militarily restricted, were sufficiently dramatic to encourage an embattled people; and this led to further adaptations of guerrilla techniques, and finally to their employment in the training, not only of elaborated and expanded "special forces," but of other troops as well.

Now, we can grant that in many situations guerrilla weapons and techniques are hard to combat by conventional means—but can we really solve any *major* military problems by adopting them ourselves on a large scale? Actually, some of the techniques are nothing but those of the footpad and the thug raised to new levels of sophistication and efficiency. They may enable a maximum realization of the potential of obsolete or irrelevant weapons in certain narrow circumstances, but the time required to train great numbers of men to the necessary pitch of perfection in their use is not justified by their relatively negligible effect on the grand military equation, and on its critical imbalance especially.

They are, in short, an attempt to remedy basic physical deficiencies by intensifying certain aspects of the nonphysical determinants, without realizing that these determinants cannot *multiply* the maximum intrinsic physical potential of the weapons involved, and without regard to whether the weapons and techniques are fundamentally relevant to the problem at hand.

This is exactly what the Japanese tried to do when they emphasized the moral over the physical to the point of denying the physical reality. It has one virtue, and that a dubious one: it is easier to train a soldier for maximum toughness than for maximum intelligence, and far easier to deny the nature of a problem than to think out an economical solution to it.

A comparison which comes to mind is the current vogue, here in the United States, for the Oriental "killing arts"—a vogue which owes much to the publicity given in the mass media to commando and guerrilla activity. A good example is *karate*, a discipline of greatly restricted modern utility (except perhaps when it is considered as a sport), and one which was developed only because the Tokugawa Shogunate had forbidden the populace of Okinawa to bear arms and had enforced the prohibition with the swords of its samurai. *Karate* takes interminable training and practice, and the fact that a good *karate* man can kill an armed opponent with his bare hands under certain circumstances scarcely compensates for the rarity with which such a need arises.

Guerrilla Warfare and the Critical Imbalance

We live in an age of unprecedented weapons, unprecedented problems, unprecedented perils—and the temptation to seek safety in symbolic strength, especially when it has a high TV entertainment value, is hard for many to resist. Yet it must be resisted, and it must be resisted with the greatest obstinacy where guerrilla warfare is concerned.

The more complex an organism is, the more vulnerable it is, however dangerous its superior development may make it. The tiger, a highly organized creature, can be killed instantly by one bullet in the heart or head. It can be crippled by a bullet in the spine. All its ferocity and power to destroy can be canceled instantly. A crocodile or shark, both lower on the evolutionary ladder, still are highly enough organized to be similarly, though less completely, vulnerable. A swarm of hornets, weaker as a multitude than any one of these, still can be much harder to fight off or to destroy. So can jungle leeches, or mindless jellyfish.

Let us define the conditions of modern guerrilla warfare before completing the analogy:

1. The terrain must at least permit, if not assist, concealment and movement of adequately large guerrilla forces.
2. The indigenous population must be cooperative enough with the guerrilla forces to conceal them, help to provision them, and assist them in the movement of supplies.
3. Guerrilla forces must receive war materiel and other assistance from allies powerful enough to give them some degree of weapons parity.
4. Counter-guerrilla forces must present objectives, and operate according to principles, which make it possible for guerrilla methods to succeed.

Without these basic conditions, guerrilla warfare would be futile except (as in so much of Europe during World War II) in active co-operation with major conventional forces actively deployed against the enemy—for these are the conditions which can prevent the achievement of a critical imbalance against guerrillas. Guerrilla armies are biologically primitive creatures. They are the white ants, the leeches, the hornets of modern war. Their nervous systems, their systems of supply and maintenance, the ways by which they move, are far less obvious and far more diffused than those of standard military forces.

Therefore, while the methods of achieving a critical imbalance—by *quantitative superiority,* by *qualitative superiority,* and by *technological surprise*—remain completely valid when applied to them, the application must be relevant to the conditions, outlined above, which make modern guerrilla warfare possible. It must take into consideration, realistically, *all* the phases of expression of both one's own M→ and the guerrilla's M′→, and of the parallel realization of his V′→ and one's own V→. In other words, we must not try to kill hornets with weapons designed to slay tigers; nor must we use them to protect ourselves against white ants or leeches. Above all, in trying to achieve a critical imbalance against guerrilla forces, we must never make the terrible error of simply copying and attempting to intensify those of *their* techniques which have succeeded against *us,* for their use of these techniques has been directly determined by the above-listed four conditions essential to guerrilla warfare, while ours must be determined by the war *against* guerrillas—that is, by those conditions indirectly, as they affect counter-guerrilla operations. To use guerrilla methods—or even super-guerrilla methods—against guerrillas must inevitably result in a tedious and expensive prolongation of the conflict, in which any favorable critical imabalance is highly unlikely.

The guerrilla actions which we must take seriously today have several characteristics in common. Generally, the terrain is either very rough or has relatively heavy cover: jungle, semi-jungle, brush, forests. Sometimes we find the two combined. Again, usually the indigenous population either have legitimate grievances against their government, their "ruling classes," or their own poverty, or—and this is the same thing—can be agitated into believing that they do. Finally, exterior sources of supply exist to provide guerrillas with modern and appropriate weapons, and often with trained political agitators and military leaders.

If these conditions are *not* present—as, for example,

where "guerrilla war" is threatened by dissident elements in our cities—there can be little real cause for concern if the authorities are willing to take prompt and relevant action, for it is relatively simple, if normal law enforcement methods fail, to cordon off an entire area and then cut off its supplies and utilities.

The ultimate $M\rightarrow$ realized by a guerrilla force is determined through the several phases of its expression just as inflexibly as is the $M\rightarrow$ of any conventional army, and no guerrilla force can be much more than an expensive nuisance if that phase chain is broken: it certainly cannot hope to achieve a critical imbalance against the less vulnerable forces of conventional authority.

The next, the final chapter of this book, will consider the problem of our optimum response to the various unprecedented military situations now confronting us, and the matter of anti-guerrilla policies and techniques will be taken up again. Here it is enough to emphasize once more that guerrilla warfare and anti-guerrilla warfare are fundamentally quite different, and that in either a critical imbalance can be achieved only by employing instruments and techniques best suited to it.

Vulnerability and the Critical Imbalance

The realization of vulnerability actually plays as crucial a part in the achievement of the unbalanced equation and the critical imbalance as does the expression of destructive force, and the rules governing M and M′ through all the phases apply, only in different terms, also to V and V′. Thus, where the determinants of M and M′ must be judged by their ultimate effect on M→ and M′→ in the weapons phases, so must the negative determinants of V and V′ be judged. It is not enough that men be killed or wounded, that ships be sunk or aircraft shot down or cities burned. Every military act must have its rationale; it should affect directly the enemy's ability to express M′ and realize V. We could, of course, examine separately the various aspects of vulnerability in each of the several phases of expression. This would seem unnecessary. Instead we can state a general principle, paralleling that governing the relevance of the instruments employed to the task in hand, namely the relevance of the objective.

The Relevance of the Objective

The relevance of the objective is determined directly by the degree to which the enemy's vulnerability values are concentrated in it—not just the *immediate* V′ of men and means, but the derivative V′→ of any and all agencies for the future expression of M′→. In other words, the objective in every instance is relevant *to the degree that the enemy's M′→ depends on it,* for it is this relationship which determines its relevance to the rest of the equation as a whole. All indecisive engagements and campaigns, examined with this principle in mind, will show—regardless of the carnage wrought—that the objective either was not highly relevant to the future development of M′→, or that its relevance was not understood and that therefore the continuity necessary to the critical imbalance was interrupted.

The relevance of the objective cannot be overemphasized. Unless it is thoroughly comprehended, men die uselessly, resources are thrown away to no purpose, and a state of war which could be successfully terminated in a short time may endure interminably. It would be possible to present innumerable examples. However, one will suffice, because it illustrates the point with such unusual clarity, and because its hard statistics are available: the "strategic bombardment" of Germany and Japan in World War II.

In *The Conduct of War,* published in 1961, J. F. C. Fuller[11] presents a concise analysis of what was and was not accomplished, basing it mainly on the *U.S. Strategic Bombing Survey* for each theater. Reproducing two charts from the *Survey,* he shows that German production of aircraft and of war materiel generally increased steadily until mid-1944, despite the fact that—

> The attacks on urban targets resulted in enormous physical damage. 'During the period from October 1939 to May 1945 the Allied Air Forces, primarily the R.A.F., dropped over one-half million tons of high explosives, incendiaries, and fragmentation bombs . . . on 61 cities . . . These cities included 25,000,000 people . . . attacks are estimated to have totally destroyed or heavily damaged 3,600,000 dwelling units, accounting for 20 per cent of Germany's total residential units, and to have rendered homeless 7,500,000 people. They killed about 300,000 people and injured some 780,000.' Berlin was estimated to be 60 to 70 per cent destroyed . . . three-fourths of the damage was caused by fire.' Although decline in morale was considerable, it had practically no effect on armament production . . . [The deletions are General Fuller's.]

Fuller also quotes the *Survey* to the effect that the destruction of buildings involved no proportionate destruction of machine tools, and that consequently the enemy was able to resume production much more rapidly than had

---

[11] Fuller, *op. cit.,* pp. 282, 285-286, 298.

been expected. However, his most telling point is made in discussing the change in bombing policy made in 1944. It is well worth quoting at length:

> . . . When preparations to invade Normandy were in progress, the question arose as to which were the most profitable targets for Bomber Command R.A.F. and the U.S. Strategic Air Force to strike at. The decision arrived at was that priority should be given to transportation and synthetic oil plants. Thus, at long last, strategic bombing became truly strategic, and the requirements Churchill had laid down in his Memorandum of 21st October 1917, were met.[12]

During the preparatory period of the invasion, the main air object was to disrupt all rail traffic between Germany and Normandy; and later, as the front moved eastward, to attack the railways and canals extending into Germany. This had a catastrophic effect on the distribution of coal. We read in the *Survey:*

'Essen Division car replacements of coal which had been 21,400 daily in January 1944 declined to 12,000 in September . . . By November deliveries of coal to factories in

---

[12] *Ibid,* pp. 279-280. General Fuller quotes at length from the Churchill Memorandum of 21 October 1917. Because I agree with General Fuller's opinion that it should not have been forgotten, I shall quote it again here: "All attacks on communications or bases should have their relation to the main battle. It is not reasonable to speak of an air offensive as if it were going to finish the war by itself. It is improbable that any terrorization of the civil population which could be achieved by air attack could compel the Government of a great nation to surrender. Familiarity with bombardment, a good system of dugouts and shelters, a strong control by police and military authorities, should be sufficient to preserve the national fighting power unimpaired. In our case we have seen the combative spirit of the people aroused, and not quelled, by the German raids. Nothing we have learned of the capacity of the German population to endure suffering justifies us in assuming that they could be cowed into submission by such methods, or, indeed, that they would not be rendered more desperately resolved by them. Therefore our offensive should consistently be directed at striking at the bases and communications upon whose structure the fighting power of his armies and his fleets of the sea and of the air must depend. Any injury which comes to the civil population from the process of attack must be regarded as incidental and inevitable."

Bavaria had been reduced by nearly 50 percent . . . By January 1945 coal placements in the Ruhr district were down to 9,000 cars per day. Finally in February well-nigh complete interdiction in the Ruhr district was obtained. Such coal as was loaded was subject to confiscation by the railroad to supply locomotive fuel coal . . . Contemporaneously, as mining continued at a higher level than transport, coal stocks at Ruhr collieries rose from 415,000 tons to 2,217,000 and coke stocks increased from 630,000 tons to 3,069,000 in the same 6 months.'

In May 1944, preliminary attacks were made on the larger synthetic oil plants, but it was not until after the Normandy landings in June that the main blow was struck. By July every major plant had been hit. In May these plants had been producing 316,000 tons a month; in June their output fell to 107,000 tons, and in September to 17,000. These attacks also dealt a crippling blow to the munitions and explosives industries, and reduced the supply of synthetic rubber, which fell to about one-sixth of its wartime peak of 12,000 tons a month.

From the above it will be seen that the air attack on Germany only became a true strategical operation when it was directed against the sources of energy and the means of distribution. From the first, had bombing been restricted to them, vast economies could have been effected, and the savings could have been invested in the production of landing craft, anti-submarine and transport aircraft, which throughout the war were in constant short supply.

The great importance of this statement is emphasized by the statistics Fuller gives for the proportion of bombs dropped on military targets (30.5), on industrial (13.5), on urban (24), and on railways, canals, and synthetic oil plants (32). This, he states, means that with military targets excluded, "A greater tonnage of bombs was dropped on secondary targets (industrial and urban) than on primary (railways and synthetic oil)."

As "England devoted 40 to 50 percent of her war production to her air forces, and the United States 35 per cent . . ." we can see at once what an enormous difference would have been made in the achievement of the unbalanced equation and the ultimate critical imbalance had the relevance of the objectives been understood earlier and the most relevant given precedence over the less relevant and the totally irrelevant.

Speaking of the strategic bombardment of Japan, Fuller has much the same sort of comment:

> . . . In the aggregate 104,000 tons of bombs were dropped on sixty-six cities, and 42,900 on industrial areas. Although this bombing reduced production, loss of shipping remained the dominant factor in Japan's economic decline, because it was the interdiction of coal, oil, other raw materials as well as grain, and not the destruction of factories and urban centres that struck the deadliest blow at her economy.
>
> The *Survey* points out that much of this bombing was duplicative, because most of the Japanese factories, oil refineries, steel mills, and munition plants lacked raw materials, and in consequence Japan's economy was in a large measure being destroyed twice over, once by cutting off imports, and secondly by air attack. Further, that attack of Japan's extremely vulnerable railroad network would have greatly extended and cumulated the effects of the shipping attack already made. 'The Survey,' we read, 'believes that such an attack [on a stated number of rail ferries, tunnels and bridges] had it been well-planned in advance, might have been initiated . . . in August 1944 . . . The Survey has estimated that the force requirements to effect complete interdiction of the railroad system would have been 650 B-29 visual sorties carrying 5,200 tons of high explosive bombs.'
>
> When these requirements are deducted from the 15,000 sorties flown and the 104,000 tons of bombs dropped on the sixty-six cities, the residue is a fair comment on the strategic error committed by the Joint Chiefs of Staff.

148   *Decisive Warfare*

Here we have two separate and major instances of vast values of M→ being expressed against adequately vulnerable but largely irrelevant objectives without achieving much toward a critical imbalance in its true sense. In the first, when new and relevant objectives are selected, we find the imbalance, or at least the conditions necessary to it, being precipitated along an accelerating curve. In the second, we find other expressions of M→ duplicating and perhaps even exceeding what is actually accomplished, while the changes to certain really relevant objectives are never made. Together, they demonstrate the principle of the relevance of the objective so vividly that no other is needed.

The Critical Imbalance and War in the Future

The true critical imbalance, deliberately created where there is an initial balance of forces, is a rare thing. Not many generals or admirals have been able to achieve it, and how we can profit from their successes and their failures will depend to a very great extent on the shape war will take. If we face a future of limited wars, then the lessons of the critical imbalance will be as urgent as they ever were. If, on the other hand, unlimited war between first-rate powers—and soon even between second- and third- and fourth-rate powers—is inevitable, then we can say that except for the remote chance of an *absolute* technological surprise, combined with a hitherto unattempted system of "civil" defense, the true critical imbalance cannot possibly be achieved.

The concept of the critical imbalance does not include a military equation which results in the total destruction of the "loser" and the two-thirds or three-quarters or nine-tenths destruction of the "winner." This may be victory to the type of mind which can contemplate with equanimity or with excitement the deliberate melting of the polar caps, the divergence of the ocean's currents, or the contrivance of a Doomsday Machine. It may be victory to the madder sort of political fanatic or man of power. Artistically, it is not a general's victory, for it is the negation of generalship. From any Western religious or humanitarian standpoint, it cannot be a victory for any sane man, civilian or military.

Because it cannot be, and because as matters stand it is impossible to discount the possibility of an all-out war, we must continue to seek means both to achieve a favorable critical imbalance and to ensure that no unfavorable critical imbalance can be achieved by any potential enemy.

It must be understood that the concept of mutual deterrence is based on the balanced equation, or at least on an equation so nearly balanced that no critical imbalance can occur and no decisive victory be attained. This is all very well when words are being juggled by physical scientists bedazzled by their new importance, by political and academic mandarins responding to the puppet-strings of their own status, by news analysts and columnists whose job it is to juggle words. There is, as I have already pointed out, one thing wrong with it: lunatics, quite a number of whom have during the past few years become the heads of sovereign states, are not always governed by the harsh realities of vulnerability and destructive force. It is only too easy for them to believe that, through their personal virtue, their national genius, the inferiority of the enemy, or the certain favor of some deity like Marx or Mao or Moloch, an instant critical imbalance can be achieved.

"It's simple. You just add heavy water."

However, this question of war in the future is highly complex. It will be considered in greater detail in the next chapter.

The Optimum Response

On the first page of chapter 1, a test of a *decisive* operation was given: "Does the war or operation achieve a prompt, conclusive victory at a minimum cost and with a minimum of wasted effort?" The question of its ultimate *political* decisiveness was deliberately excluded. This chapter (while retaining the definition, which serves our purpose here as well as in the other chapters) will touch at least occasionally on that excluded question, because *indecisive* operations—a category which must include, not only the failure to act adequately, but sometimes the failure to act at all—often cannot be properly evaluated unless the matter of *political decisiveness* is taken into account.

Here we are going to consider the possibilities, if any, for

The ideal of the critical imbalance must never be forgotten, and no second-best solution should ever be accepted until, and unless, events inexorably force such a course. In many situations, naturally, no critical imbalance can be achieved, but if we always aim for it, then we will at least achieve an optimum response in terms of the military equations confronting us, and their values of destructive force, of vulnerability, and of time. We will then do the best we can, not just where courage and determination are concerned, but against the situational realities that dictate possibilities and limitations.

decisive operations in the future, and especially those possibilities as they involve the United States. We shall discuss certain of the major military problems which confront us, as well as our possible responses to them, functional and non-functional, relevant and irrelevant, always keeping in mind the ideal of the critical imbalance and of decisive action, and, in terms of this ideal, seeking the optimum response in every situation.

In the days before the technologically determined values of M and M' began escalating so rapidly, it was usually possible to discuss such matters without referring to questions of national policy. Today—except perhaps in the area of minor tactics—it is virtually impossible to write about the theory of war or about its practice in the future, without doing so. Military action only implements national policy, but often the chances for the success or failure of the action are themselves determined largely by the policy, by the domestic and foreign political and economic forces which have influenced its development, and by the international environment which it has itself helped to shape.

Of necessity, therefore, certain aspects of national policy must be considered in this chapter. As nearly as possible, the consideration will be purely military. It will be derived from and dictated by the theoretical framework already outlined in this book, and will be applied to those future military operations which now seem most probable. This, at least, is the intention. If the criticisms and opinions expressed are unjustified by the theory or by my interpretation of it, if any purely personal bias results in misstatements of fact or mistaken conclusions, then I can only ask the reader to accept my apologies.

The Decision to Use Force

The first problem we must consider is the very basic one of *whether, when, and how to employ military force,* for our response to it must inevitably determine many of the values of the resulting equations. We have, since the time of Theodore Roosevelt, when things were somewhat different, developed an uncanny flair for inadequate and indecisive action, or even for no action at all when action would seem imperative. This is a weakness which we have shared with the entire liberal West. The Russian Civil War provided one of the first examples of it; we and our Allies, had we been willing to throw in enough divisions on the side of the liberal democracy which the Communists were trying to overthrow, might have ended the Communist adventure then and there; instead, we sent in only enough troops to make the Communists hate us even more than they already did. The liberal West failed similarly when Japan launched her campaign of conquest in China proper and Manchuria, when Hitler went into the Rhineland, when Mussolini invaded Ethiopia, when Soviet Russia committed aggression against Finland, and when the Nazis took the Sudetenland and absorbed Austria.

We ourselves perpetrated somewhat similar errors when, after the Second War, we supported the idea of instant independence for any and all colonies, and thereby abetted the Communist campaign to break up the empires of our closest allies. There have been other instances: Eisenhower's deference to the Russians in the 1958 Suez Crisis; our failure to support Chiang Kai-shek with major force when the Communists were driving him out of mainland China; our not only permitting, but actually assisting Castro to take over Cuba—apparently without even suspecting his politics; and, above all, our failure in 1945 to seize the opportunity offered by our massive presence in Europe and our then atomic monopoly to institute and enforce a sane world order.

Time after time, over the years, our reluctance to undertake the limited and sane use of force has led us, later, into a situation where an unlimited, uneconomic use of force is literally forced upon us. We hesitate, shocked at the notion of losing twenty thousand men and a few hundred million dollars in a preventive operation—and less than a generation later we must lose ten times as many men and dollars by the billions to achieve the same result. We hesitate, not wanting to interfere in the affairs of a friendly but fouled-up government—and ten years later we must send our men and spend our billions either to bolster up that government or to reverse a revolution hostile to us.

We of the liberal West have been completely inconsistent in our attitude towards the use of force. Would it not have been better for France and Britain to have challenged and fought Hitler over the Rhineland than to wait, and watch the fall of France, and endure the Battle of Britain, the bombardment of London, the humiliation of Vichy, and all the rest? Would it not have been more humane to kill off a few regiments of the Reichswehr in 1933 than three hundred thousand German civilians by air bombardment a decade or so later—or allow Hitler to murder six million Jews and Slavs and members of other nationalities in his death camps? Would it not have been at once more sensible and more civilized to have destroyed Japan's naval power and, if necessary, her merchant marine, in the early 'thirties—which our industrial supremacy would have enabled us to do as well then as later—than to have waited for Pearl Harbor and the invasion of the Philippines, Java, New Guinea and Malaya, for Attu and Leyte and Iwo Jima and Kwajalein, for the fire raids on Tokyo, for Hiroshima and Nagasaki?

Jehovah's Witnesses are at least consistent regarding the use of force; they renounce it utterly. We abjure it verbally until we feel that its employment is inevitable, and then, rather than using it for the express purpose of achieving a favorably unbalanced equation and a consequently swift decision, we all too often allow ourselves to fall into one or the other of two traps. The first of these is a "war by inadequate accretion," where force is added a little here and a little there, permitting the enemy to respond in kind, and allowing a vast equation to build up where initially there might have been a much less consequential one. The second is "total" war, where emotion rather than good sense compels us to employ wasteful, unrestrained, and frequently irrelevant violence.

Granted, in both cases public apathy or fear, domestic political expediency, and established foreign policies extraneous to the issue at hand can, and do, prevent decisive action.

However, if the military principles involved were ever clearly and generally understood, the influence of these factors might at least be diminished. Force must always be employed for a defined purpose. Enough force should always be employed for the achievement of a critical imbalance with relation to that purpose, and that force should always be employed in such a manner that this critical imbalance can be achieved. The optimum response, in any given situation, is the response which will come closest to achieving that ideal.

It may be argued that the use of force is always wrong, and that therefore he who resorts to force only when he literally is driven to it is less wrong than he who, foreseeing that contingency, employs force to forestall it. From that argument follows another curious one: that, hoping to do as little harm as possible, we should initially use as little force as possible, adding to it only as we are compelled to— as neat a prescription for long and costly and indecisive warfare as one can imagine.

We would do better to ask ourselves the fundamental question: *Do we or do we not use force?* Then, if the answer is affirmative, we should enunciate a doctrine governing its use, so that we, at least, do not mistake our own intentions. That doctrine can be simply stated: *when we use force, we will endeavor to use force decisively.* It is an excellent doctrine, but it carries an inevitable corollary: that if we cannot make war decisively we will not make war at all—except, of course, when we are literally compelled to.

The main point is that we must never condone failure, never settle for second best ahead of the event; to do so is to engineer, if not our own defeat, then at least our failure to attain a victory.

Technology and the Optimum Response

Today's weapons and instruments—and, even more, tomorrow's (some of which may well, behind the veils of secrecy, exist today)—force us to contemplate, and plan for, several different types of wars:

1. *Unlimited wars between superpowers*, in which all available weapons are employed without restraint.
2. *Limited wars between superpowers*, in which, by mutual agreement stated or unstated, no weapons of ultimate destruction are employed.
3. *Unlimited wars between second- or third-rate powers*, in which available super weapons are used without restraint but in numbers inadequate to procure ultimate destruction.
4. *Limited wars between such powers, or between minor powers lacking super weapons.*
5. *Civil wars*, with or without outside intervention, limited by necessity and by their nature.

Were one to be asked now what the chances are of fighting a war of the first category decisively, one would have to answer almost without hesitation, *none*. (This, of course, is predicated on the use of the author's definition of the word *decisive*, not on one provided by our Doomsday Machinists.) When we consider that a single ICBM strike today would liberate more raw destructive force than has been expressed in all man's wars since time began—when we consider, too, that no major power has taken any truly realistic measures to cut down vulnerability values in proportion to this rise in potential M—we can see that, at least on the face of it, the prospects for a grand critical imbalance are not bright.

We must consider, first, *weapons of mass destruction:* missiles with fusion warheads delivered suborbitally or from orbit, and "multi-megaton" hydrogen mines delivered by submarines, fishing trawlers, or whatever. Two can play at that game, and there would seem to be no *decisive* future in it—though we are far more vulnerable to mines than are our most likely enemies.

Then we must consider mass destruction weapons not as well publicized but generally known either to exist or to be in the process of development: biological warfare agents, chemical agents of all sorts, and (if not today, tomorrow) ray weapons—such things as continuous wave lasers. Here again, the "two can play" rule enters the picture; though it by no means precludes the use of such devices, it may well act as a restraint—at least as long as the enemy's corresponding capacity is unknown.

Next we have the entire question of *"anti-weapon" weapons,* of weapons designed primarily not to express M, but to prevent the expression of M'. In order for such devices to be in any way decisive, there would have to be a fantastic discrepancy between those deployed by one side and by the other. It is easily conceivable that, if we put our reliance solely on weight of warheads, precisely such a situation may arise, and we may find ourselves on the wrong side of a very critical imbalance indeed; we may hope, however, that no one in authority will be so negligent of sense and duty as to permit such a thing to happen.

Actually, the subject of "anti-weapon" weapons is not quite so simple, for it leads us directly to another class of weapons altogether: completely unexpected weapons, whose advent is not heralded by open scientific progress, or by normal scientific extrapolation from the already known. A "counter-missile" weapon in this class could quite easily be shatteringly decisive. It would be pointless, here, to speculate at any length either on the possibilities inherent in such weapons or on the directions their exploration or development might take. But it seems obvious that today there is an unprecedented employment of the scientific method by a fantastic diversity of peoples for a fantastic diversity of purposes, under unprecedented conditions of "security" which not only enable research and development in secret but also, because of the restrictions they put on specialists, inhibit *defensive* speculation.

Such unanticipated weapons might provide the one means by which a grand critical imbalance could be achieved in first category wars—the absolute technological surprise, the surprise which (as in a perfect "anti-missile" weapon) might nullify the enemy's capacity to strike, or else (as in a weapon of complete and instant saturation) might destroy completely his hardened capacity to retaliate. Weapons of this sort are not impossible; they are just unlikely—though the "counter-missile" weapons may be less unlikely than the rest of them.

Wars of the second category—limited wars directly between super powers—seem at this writing to be highly improbable. Any nation or alliance launching such a war would be doing so for one purpose only—to upset the present structure and balance of the world—and would thereby be inviting, and making virtually inevitable, that unlimited escalation which automatically would make a critical imbalance impossible, if not immediately, then at the point where one side or the other would seem certain of decisive victory. Let us put it this way: if Hitler, at the last, could have pushed a big red button in the Führerbunker and blown his enemies and Germany alike to Kingdom Come, he would almost certainly have done so.

Wars of the third category—unlimited wars between second- and third-rate states—are a very recently-developed possibility, regarding which there has been little speculation. However, as there are a number of nuclear powers today without a saturation capacity, such wars must at least be considered

Let us consider an interesting, if slightly far-fetched, example. Suppose that Charles de Gaulle, tomorrow, decided to proclaim himself Emperor of China—or, conversely, that Chairman Mao, finally overwhelmed by the profundity of his own thought, announced to the world that he was now the fourth Napoleon. Either of these gentlemen would have fusion bombs to drop upon the other. However, except to those Chinese or Frenchmen unfortunate enough to be there if and when they hit, the bombs could not be in any way decisive; neither nation would have enough of a preponderance to ensure a critical imbalance, though France, because of her much smaller area, would be at something of a disadvantage.

Again, were powers of this class to employ super weapons of a different sort—biologicals, let us say—against each other or against greater powers, they would be asking for massive intervention either by the superpowers or by coalitions of their own equals. At the moment, unlimited wars of this category do not seem too probable—though, if one considers the incidence of megalomania in high office, or the recent political behavior of the Chinese, the odds against them do seem less favorable.

Wars of the fourth category—limited wars between major powers lacking a saturation capacity or between powers lacking super weapons—would seem to be considerably more likely to occur, with the likelihood increasing where super weapons are completely absent. Such wars, if they do not bring an outside super weapon intervention, can indeed be militarily decisive—as the Israeli-Arab War of 1967 demonstrated very clearly. We can expect more of them, for we and the British and the French, abdicating the responsibilities of true world leadership (or, if you will, of empire), have played the Russian game of arming, not only small civilized nations, but also nations composed almost entirely of savages or of illiterate, easily-manipulated mobs. The Russians and Chinese have had a purpose in this: to sow discord and to reap its harvest of revolutionary overthrow. Our purpose, presumably, has been to prevent this, but we have made the error of arming without reforming, of giving without imposing strict conditions, of trying to buy the fealty of grasping, unscrupulous, and often thoroughly incompetent native leaders, too many of whom have rewarded us with active anti-American policies and propaganda—and in many cases, even after this has become obvious, we have continued to finance our own betrayal and to provide the engines for attacks against our allies. Regardless of the emotional slogans of small nationalism, this fragmentation of an unprepared world has resulted in less, rather than more, individual freedom for the peoples of the new-born nations, and has multiplied many times the potential military problems facing the United States. The situation makes a lot of sense to the revolutionary Left, in the United States itself and throughout the world. But it makes no sense at all where our national security and survival are concerned. While it is probably too late to reverse the trend and undo the damage done, we should at least take a somewhat harder stand.

We should arm our friends. We should be sure they *are* our friends before we arm them. We should *make* sure that they are honest enough and well-enough trained to use the arms we pay for—or any other American aid—effectively. Then we should arm them to the point where they at least have a chance of winning any fourth-category war decisively.

Wars of the fifth category—civil wars, rebellions, revolutions, guerrilla wars—*should probably never be called wars at all.* To call them wars dignifies them and appears to legitimatize them. They should be considered police actions, and —even when the full force of the military is employed in fighting them—they should remain police actions, and the military role, no matter how massive, should be that of a police auxiliary, as it was in the successful British operation against Communist guerrillas in Malaya.

It is always the revolutionist who profits by the breaking of this rule. At home, our mass media have given unearned status to our tiny minority of race-war agitators by going along with the Castro-Peking-Kremlin line and calling their criminal activities "rebellion" and "revolt." (They have similarly dignified the goings-on of drug addicts, motorcycle gangs, "hippies," and other spectacularly useless delinquents and malcontents.) And what the mass media have done at home, our own government and others have only too frequently done abroad.

Naturally, any attempt to fit wars or any other human phenomena into categories is bound to be only relatively accurate. In the list below we have tried to classify possible wars very largely by the M→ potential likely to be expressed in them, and this in turn has been based on the destructive force now obviously available to organized governments. The one exception has been with regard to wars of the fifth category, where we find organized governments opposed either by spontaneous and independent dissident groups or—and this is much more likely nowadays— by such groups sponsored and armed by hostile powers. From what we know of potential M and M' today, we can hazard a generalized summary regarding the likelihood of decisive action in each of the categories:

1. That no power can achieve a critical imbalance in a first category war without an *absolute* technological surprise, and that consequently a decisive war, while perhaps not impossible, is highly unlikely in this category;
2. That, while a critical imbalance can probably be achieved in a second category war, the probability that its achievement will automatically convert the war into a first category affair will almost certainly prevent it from being decisive;
3. That a critical imbalance and a decisive war are highly unlikely but still possible in the third category;
4. That in the fourth and fifth categories a critical imbalance and a decisive war are not only still possible but are quite likely *unless* there is interference by exterior major powers.

The simple truth of the matter is that, as things stand, unless one side does achieve a thoroughly improbable absolute technological surprise, any equation for a first category war will for all practical purposes spell out the mutual destruction of the combatants and of much of the rest of the world as well. Here is the reasonable basis for "deterrence," and if all men were reasonable we could rely on it to prevent all major wars, not just in the first category, but at least in the second and third as well.

But *not* all men are reasonable, and the accelerating curves of scientific "progress" do *not* stand still, and no group of men has an assured monopoly on the devices of destructive force. Therefore we are compelled to consider *all* the inevitable curves of increasing M→, *all* the diverse groups which may conceivably secure control of its new instruments, and *all* the dreams, ambitions and beliefs—however alien to our own—which may motivate them.

We must consider these for two good reasons: first, so that we may, if possible, organize the world to prevent wars, especially those in the upper categories; and second, failing that, so that we can at least try to prepare ourselves to fight decisively rather than just destructively if war is forced upon us.

Science, Destructive Force and Decisive Action

C. P. Snow and a great many other thinkers have commented on the widening intellectual gap between the physical scientist and his contemporaries trained either in the "social sciences" or the humanities. Generally the reasoning goes pretty much as follows: During the Renaissance, there were many "universal men," like Leonardo, who knew virtually everything there was to be known at the time, men who were at once scientists, philosophers, theologians, engineers, artists, and men of action. Today, with the "knowledge explosion" of the past two centuries, such men are no longer possible, for there is too much to be learned, too much to be remembered, too much to be comprehended. Now we have only specialists, and the more we know as a race, the less universal men must get, for the more our specialists learn about their ever-more-complicated fields, the less they are bound to know about everything in general.

This, of course, is facile thinking, the first-glance plausibility of which conceals its fundamental error. An intimate knowledge of thermonuclear physics, or of any other esoteric field, is no more necessary to an understanding of where the scientific method is taking this world of ours than skill in swimming is necessary to a career in oceanography. All that is needed is that a person be generally well-read (which many specialists aren't), that he know something of epistemology (which most specialists don't), and that he have some comprehension of how the scientific method works when enough people use it and enough money is provided for its use. This is extremely simple: the curve of scientific progress is a geometrical progression, the steepness of which depends directly on the quantity and quality of men and means provided.

Where weapons are concerned, this means that we have long since entered a period when the intensity of destructive force is increasing along such a curve, when the areas of expression of destructive force are expanding along such a curve, when the availability of the instruments of destructive force must increase and their cost decline along related curves, and when the compensatory values of vulnerability in the equations of war *must* be adjusted to conform to an analogous negative curve. Remember, the curve of scientific progress is open-ended. If a weapon, say, reaches the peak of its development, that is not the end; almost invariably a new and superior weapon will take over and, as its own curve steepens, surpass it. Again, there is no theoretical lower limit on availability and cheapness. We have already heard serious fears expressed about the possibility of criminal and subversive groups acquiring nuclear weapons,[1] and we have now reached the point—perhaps of no return— where the accelerating proliferation of nuclear and other "super-weapons" is assured, treaty with Russia or no treaty. The French and the Chinese have made this point quite clear.

Such a treaty follows along with the whole philosophy

---

[1] An Associated Press dispatch released in Washington and printed in the San Francisco *Chronicle*, May 18, 1967, states:

"An Atomic Energy Commission advisory panel has cautioned that a 'black market' is likely to develop in fissionable materials, with criminal or terrorist groups attempting to divert the materials into secret production of atomic weapons.

"To prevent such production of atomic weapons, the panel recommended intensified efforts to develop an effective, universal safeguard system as well as severe criminal penalties for diversification of fissionable materials.

"It is also proposed that an informer system be set up with rewards provided. . . ."

of "disarmament," which has been a carrot-on-a-stick for eighty years and more. You cannot *disarm* a technological society even if wants to be disarmed. Weapons are only instruments of power, and innumerable instruments of power not designed specifically as weapons can become weapons in a moment, in an hour, or overnight. When does the gasoline in an auto's tank become a firebomb? When does the caterpillar tractor become a tank, or the weedburner a flamethrower? Where does the jet transport end and the stratospheric bomber begin? Where does the laboratory for bacteriological research turn into one for biological warfare research? As instruments of power constantly become more powerful, more readily available, and less expensive, questions such as these become more pressing, and it is by no means too early now to consider seriously the problems of control which will arise when super weapons of, say, city-busting capacity become available to determined and resourceful small groups, or even individuals. For instance, once the remaining difficulties delaying the development of continuous-wave lasers have been solved—and they will be solved—it will be just another step to the continuous wave laser constructed in a basement workshop, if not by the "mad scientist" of popular entertainment, then by some "dedicated expert". The choice seems academic.

This is one of the too-immediate problems of our age, which we simply are not facing. If we extrapolate only those weapons curves which are now obvious, it at once becomes apparent that planning either for a stable world or for decisive warfare will be extremely difficult and extremely challenging during the next few years. The first will demand an unprecedented level of imagination and political acumen; the prediction of its future is not within the province of this book. The second will be no less demanding, and here we can perhaps be hopeful, for our military now appear to be more intellectually active than ever before.

Planning
the Optimum
Response

Ideally, one should either plan decisive wars or plan decisively for no wars at all. The latter we have not done, for the United Nations has almost all the faults and weaknesses of the old League of Nations, plus some peculiarly its own. The world, instead of being unified, has been turned into a "super-Balkans", multiplying the possibilities and potentialities for war fantastically. Therefore it behooves us to consider the first alternative very seriously, so that, always aiming for the ideal of decisive war, we will be able to achieve at least the optimum response dictated by any military equation with which we are confronted.

It should, of course, be completely obvious to intelligent men that first and second category wars, as instruments of national policy, have become senseless and suicidal, and that even third and sometimes (when intervention threatens) fourth category wars run the risk of instant escalation. Were anyone to suggest seriously today that modern infantry should form up shoulder to shoulder in ranks three deep, and then, at a word of command, fire their automatic weapons at each other at a range of fifty yards, he would quite rightly be considered crazy. Yet this is precisely what is now being threatened on the Great Power level, for we have run out of adequate room for dispersal, and adequate interposition is generally considered impracticable. Powers with a saturation ballistic missile capability are precisely in the position of those duelists who, in the Old South, are reputed to have fought occasionally with shotguns across a card table.

Unfortunately, we now seem stuck with it, at least as far ahead as we can see. It would take as long to reorient and redirect the world's foreign policies as it would to re-educate the men who made them; it would be necessary to persuade the Russians, the Chinese, and God alone knows who else. Reality, and especially that part of it which comprehends the processes of war, tells us that today any all-out conflict between first-rate powers must, to all intents and purposes, *be* a Doomsday Machine. But all men do not follow the same map of reality, of structure and process, and they believe not what reality predicts, but what their maps tell them.

Marx, when he wrote *Das Kapital*, derived his map of human affairs partly from the philosophies and sciences *of his day*, partly from his own observations of contemporary societies, and partly from the observations of others in the past. The desire to find order in the world so that we can predict and control events is natural to human intelligence; unhappily, it is also natural to us to attempt to impose imagined order *on* the world, insisting that this map *is* the reality. The Marxist map is an example. Phenomena which did not fit it, Marx either ignored, flatly denied, or side-tracked with specious explanations. Most of his followers are still doing it today. Therefore the Marxist map, with additions and subtractions and alterations by Lenin, Stalin, Mao, and a host of miscellaneous theorists, is no more accurate now than it was a hundred years ago. It is, if any-thing, far less reliable as a guide through the fantastic scientific wilderness in which we live. But most of its exponents do not see this. The Chinese general, the Chinese scientist, the Red Guard juvenile delinquent, dutifully chanting the Marxist thoughts of Mao, cannot see that these thoughts can do nothing to mitigate the fury of atomic fusion. Many Vietnamese or Cuban or Russian Communist intellectuals, because their maps show otherwise, cannot believe that a vast majority of American workingmen are totally disinterested in revolution.

And it is not only the Marxist map with which we need to be concerned. Hitler's was different, but it was quite as wrong as theirs. The map of causes and effects in the mind of a tribal African, a Hindu Kali-worshipper, or a Japanese follower of Soku Gakkai—all these are very different from our own. Sooner or later, we may be forced to consider any or all of them. Finally, because no map is ever *wholly* accurate, we should constantly reassess and reform our own —for, while we may not be able to prevent others from making great mistakes, we can at least restrain ourselves from making them.

At the moment, then, we have no choice but to plan for the eventuality of war; and good sense dictates that, regardless of its category, we should plan if possible to fight decisively.

How can we do this?

First, we should initiate a hard reëvaluation of all our military prospects from the standpoint of the equations of war—the standpoint of potential $M\rightarrow$ and $M'\rightarrow$, $V\rightarrow$ and $V'\rightarrow$, and their determinants. We must reëvaluate existing weapons, instruments, and instrumentalities. We must reëvaluate their capabilities in each of the several phases of expression, as well as their potential in wars of every category. This reëvaluation should always contribute to the dual purpose of achieving a favorable critical imbalance and preventing any enemy from achieving an unfavorable one. It should be a continuing process, a normal day-by-day staff function. Specifically, it should find and ruthlessly eliminate obsolete and obsolescent weapons and agencies. It should similarly find and eliminate techniques of dubious military effectiveness—regardless of their symbolic or emotional appeal. It should, wherever possible, seek to simplify—for complexity and specialization divide strength, while simplicity and functional generalization (if no serious loss of specific efficiency ensues) tend to enable its maximum realization. However, it should distinguish very clearly the simple from the simplistic, the truly simple from the falsely so. It should focus every aspect of the preparation of force towards one goal: the favorable critical imbalance and decisive war.

Secondly, we should reassess every category of war from the standpoint not only of the determinants of M and V as they now exist, but as they will in all probability exist a year from now, or two years, or five. We should decide which categories can still be useful instruments of policy and which can not.

Thirdly, we should, having done this, revise our foreign policy in accordance with our findings. There never was a time when force, in principle, could be the tool of policy and nothing more—though often, when force seemed overwhelming, it has in practice played such a role. Today, more than ever in the past, the facts of force and vulnerability become determinants of policy, and if we intend to survive and to prevail we must recognize this both in principle and practice. Especially must we do so in those spheres which concern the organization and policing of the world. Any world organization, even a ramshackle assortment of unenforced alliances, must—if it is to stand any chance at all of being successful—be based, not on hope, but on the realities of power.

Fourthly, we should make every effort to close the contemporary gap between men of policy and military commanders. Many years have passed since the days when kings could and often did play either one role or the other, and a quite unnecessary disadvantage of subordinating the military to the civil authority has been the "walling-off" of one from the other by increased specialization, if not of function, at least of background and of vested interest. The man of policy today too often considers the military estab-lishment merely as a tool to serve his purposes, never be-coming intimate with military history and military theory, but trusting to his specialists as blindly as most men trust their airline pilots or their surgeons. Sometimes, too, to-day's military man, properly avoiding involvement in what the Constitution says is not his business, can carry his de-tachment a step too far and become too dedicated an in-strument, ignorant of the concerns of policy except as they affect him in this narrow context. Needless to say, we are arguing here, not for military government, not for a heavy military influence in government, but for a return to some measure of Renaissance universality among men who gov-ern and those who command the armed forces which serve government. Clemenceau may have been right when he said that war is much too important a business to be en-trusted to generals, but one can say with at least equal justice that national policy is too important, and nowadays much too risky, to be entrusted solely to politicians.

Fifthly, so that we may be spared the necessity for fight-ing a Doomsday-Machine war—the most completely in-decisive of all wars—we should start to explore new ways of planning decisively for a world without war. Our re-sponse to this problem has been far less than optimum; it has been quite non-functional. We should abandon our foolish and futile efforts to abolish war by outlawing the instruments with which we wage it, for it is *we* who wage war, not these instruments. Guns don't kill people. People kill people. This is true of guns, of H-bombs—of poison. It is even true of Doomsday Machines, conceived by dedi-cated experts. In eighty years of the search after disarma-ment, war after terrible war has been fought, and exactly *nothing* has been accomplished. It is time we tried for different solutions, for more positive and realistic ways of keeping the peace.

We should begin by redefining the word *disarmament*. If it can mean only the legal outlawing of instruments of power, then the cause is lost. But if we use it as an ordnance man would, when he speaks of *disarming* a live bomb, then we can hope again. We could, for instance, try to convert the feeble instrumentalities of peace into more effective agencies.

Strangely, a professional soldier, and one often damned as a militarist by the Liberal Left—General Douglas MacArthur—suggested one very simple, very practical method, which was incorporated in the new Japanese Constitution. He had observed that those nations which, like Switzerland and Uruguay, had denounced war *in their own constitutions* had never gone to war, and he suggested that *all* nations should do likewise, for one's own basic law is more binding than any treaty. Actually, there is no reason why the outlawing of war by domestic law should not be made a condition for membership in the United Nations, or indeed for any form of international recognition or intercourse. However, I have never heard of any statesman anywhere paying any heed to General MacArthur's proposal.

Actually, where peace and war are concerned, mankind is faced with three alternatives. The first is the outlawing of *all* force in the settlement of international disputes. The second, on which we seem at least temporarily to have settled, is a balance of terror which allows only the peripheral use of force. The third, which I have not seen seriously suggested, is an admission that the urge to violence is inherent in human nature, and a general agreement to engage in limited warfare under universally accepted rules and conditions; if this has psychological validity, the objection that it would be as easy to prohibit war completely may be less cogent than it appears to be.

The scientific method, the exercise of which has been responsible for our present dilemma of policy and power, is also working other changes in our situation, one or another of which may cause us, if we are lucky, to alter our direction rather rapidly. Foremost among these is the fact that we are adventuring into space. We ourselves have barely pushed our heads out of the atmosphere in which we were evolved, but our devices have already circled Mars and crashed on Venus, and more are on the way. It is a matter of time only until men stand upon this alien ground, until we voyage out to see the rings of Saturn and touch the moons of Jupiter. These are the first short steps—far shorter than the first steps of a Himalayan tribesman who leaves his native village to see the myriad mysteries of the world. The universe is so vast, so unknown, that the few data our poor instruments have gathered tell us almost nothing of it. We have no way of knowing what or whom we may encounter as we extend our explorations and make our presence known. It is unfortunate that man should undertake this great adventure still disunited and at daggers drawn. However, it would be difficult to persuade Kosygin of this, to say nothing of convincing Mao, or Papa Doc, or Gamal Abdel Nasser.

As things stand, we are stuck, at least for the time being, with our uneasy and inherently unstable balance of terror, and—failing such sane approaches as MacArthur's—presumably we must make the best of it. The way to do that is, I think, not to attempt to terrorize the enemy, but to make certain that any military equation will—if it is humanly possible—be unbalanced, and critically unbalanced, in our favor.

The Optimum Response: M and Its Instruments

The ideal response, of course, is one which results in a

favorable critical imbalance. However, there obviously are a great many cases in which the values of the equation physically do not permit its achievement; here the optimum response is the closest approach to the ideal which can be attained under the circumstances. This must be admitted, just as the physical fact of vulnerability must be admitted —but in every instance it must finally be accepted *only with great reluctance and as a last resort.* The evolution of tactics and techniques has shown innumerable examples of what had always been an optimum response rendered sadly suboptimum by a new idea, a new method, a new instrument, a new expedient. Witness the cavalry of Asia and of Europe confronted by the Mongols; infantry in mass first facing breech-loading rifles; air forces trained to a turn-around time of 10x trying to outdo an enemy trained to a time one fifth of that. We should always seek to achieve this sort of upset, never until the last moment admitting that we cannot. In order to be in a position to do so, especially in this age of rapid technological development and the threat of technological surprise, it is necessary to evaluate the potentialities of M and its instruments with special care *before the event.* No response can be considered optimum if sub-optimum means are voluntarily chosen and employed.

We have already discussed the subject of the evaluation of weapons and instrumentalities in terms of the military equation. However, it may be interesting to speculate further on certain specific weapons and classes of weapons, beginning with the increasingly important and vexing problem of their simplification. The proliferation of "special purpose" instruments for the expression of M through its several phases has become fantastic, and has increased the complexity of administration and supply quite as fantastically. Anyone wishing an instant visual picture of this should compare the present editions of the *Staff Officers' Field Manual* with their pre-World War II counterparts.

This complexity, naturally, has fostered the growth of bureaucracy, and—as complexity and bureaucracy always do—has increased the factor of probable error all along the line. As a consequence, simplification is much to be desired if it can be attained without significantly diminishing M→ or increasing V→. It must always be remembered that complexity and specialization tend to divide total M, and that by rendering the whole more critically dependent on its parts, they tend to multiply potential V.

Where the mechanical instruments of force are concerned, simplification can best be achieved by widening their interchangeability of function, and on a different level their interchangeability of components (which, in principle, is pretty much the same thing). More has been done about the second than about the first. Our goal should be to make sure that as many military instruments and instrumentalities as possible contribute as directly as possible to the expression of M→ in its final phases. If we have a dozen vehicles, each wearing a different weight of armor, each mounting weapons of different capabilities, some specialized to bulldoze field fortifications or dig holes, others for reconnaissance or troop transport, they will, *as a force*, be weaker and more vulnerable than another dozen consisting, six and six, of heavily armored and armed vehicles capable of acting either in an assault or artillery capacity *or* as construction or demolition equipment, and of others lightly armed and armored and able to function either in scouting or troop transport, or as light combat vehicles.

In this age of radiation, chemical, and bacteriological weapons, the development of armor is a paramount consideration in preparing for land warfare—armor not only against conventional weapons, but against all these as well —and we should do our best to evolve "tanks" as militarily universal as possible. To do this, we must first liberate them from the three curses of modern armor: limited power (because of the internal combustion engine), limited range (because of the dependence of the internal combustion engine on a wasteful and vulnerable fuel supply), and limited versatility in the field (dictated largely by design considerations resulting from the other two). Our goal, I think, must be ultimately to develop light nuclear power for armored vehicles; then we could indeed combine the heavy assault, artillery, and construction functions on the one hand, and the reconnaissance, light combat, troop transport, and perhaps even supply functions on the other. As an interim measure, we should urgently develop the high-pressure steam engine and generator for armored vehicle propulsion; this would give us terrific torque at low r.p.m., a completely stall-proof engine, far fewer working parts, and an installation readily convertible if an adequately light and compact nuclear power source came along. It is interesting to contemplate an armored force almost as independent of its bases and its supply as a modern fleet at sea. Properly designed, it would be far less vulnerable to modern weapons—whether "tactical" nuclear weapons, airborne bacteria, or gas molecules—than would any unarmored adversary, at least if that adversary has any intention of remaining mobile.

In view of the possibly temporary nature of many types of manned combat aircraft, in the air we would perhaps be wise to concentrate especially on specialized aviation to cooperate closely with armor, on fighter aircraft to provide cover for that armor, and on attack and bombardment aircraft to interdict the expression of M' in its logistics phase.

At sea, our problems of weapon and instrument evaluation will almost certainly involve vulnerability more than they will destructive force, and therefore this will be discussed a page or two later.

The Optimum
Response: V
and its Values

As we have seen, M and V do not exist separately in the
military equation; each is simply one or the other side of the
whole coin, and any consideration of one automatically involves some consideration of the other. Therefore this heading represents, not a break in the discussion, but a continua-
tion of it, with only this difference: that primary emphasis
will be placed on the negative rather than the positive
aspect.

Vulnerability, unrecognized or underestimated, can prevent the attainment of an optimum response quite as effec-
tually, and quite as subtly, as any deficiency or misdirection
of M. The word *subtly* is used here because, while the factors responsible for absolute defeat draw attention to themselves and are often readily apparent, those which merely
delay or prevent victory are harder to pin down *even after
the event,* and frequently either go ignored or become
bones of endless contention. Therefore their accurate evaluation in peacetime can be of critical importance.

A word here parenthetically. Many of the opinions regarding weapons and instruments already offered in this
study have been, in the curious terminology of our day,
"controversial." When this word is used, unfortunately, it
usually means that, with regard to the subject in question,
one opinion is as good as another; that the disputants are
too emotionally involved to be reasonable; that, because
no positive point of view can be presented without hurting
feelings or imperiling interests, no attempt should be made
to present one. Not many years ago, the horse and sword
were "controversial." So, in a very different way, were the
machine gun and the military aircraft. Where these were

concerned, as a matter of fact, there never was any legitimate controversy: those authorities who defended the horse and sword were wrong; those who advocated the machine gun and the aircraft were right. The reasons, in terms of all the factors of the military equation, are now too obvious for argument. Similarly, in the author's opinion, the reasons for the arguments already proposed and to be proposed a little later, with regard to the weapons and instruments of today and tomorrow, derive directly from these factors and from the body of theory outlining them. Some of these arguments may be wrong through errors of deduction or reasoning. Science and technology may prove others to have been erroneous forecasts. But at present the author believes them to be largely right, and this belief does not imply any lack of respect for those who think otherwise.

At any rate, it would seem logical that *at sea we should do everything we can to disperse concentrations of vulnerability and to take advantage of the natural cover offered by fathoms of water.* This means, of course, that very large vessels—whether ships of war or cargo carriers—should be phased out as soon as possible, and that every effort should be made to replace them with smaller vessels, and especially *submersibles,* in both categories. If we have to fight any sort of major war overseas, our problems of supply and transport will be very different from those we faced in World War II, and we have, unhappily, done little or nothing to solve them. We have allowed our active merchant marine to melt away or, serving interests not precisely those of the United States, to escape to foreign registry. Of the newer ships, many are being designed and built with no thought for anything but immediate profit. A recent article in the *Proceedings* of the United States Naval Institute[2]

---

[2] Lewis, Captain T. L., "Canals and Channels, a Look Ahead," in *Proceedings,* United States Naval Institute, Vol. 93, No. 8. August 1967, pp. 33-43.

gives us some idea of what the future holds:

> . . . The tanker *Idemitsu Maru,* [its author writes] launched in Japan in 1966, is rated at 205,000 deadweight tons. She is 1,177.5 feet long, with a beam of 161.85 feet and her full load draft is 56 feet. More recently, in September 1966, two Japanese shipyards announced that they were awarded contracts worth $120 million by an American company for six 276,000-ton super tankers. The ships will be the largest vessels ever built. The contract from the National Bulk Carriers, Inc. is the largest ship export contract ever obtained by Japan.

The article then goes on to forecast the probable increase in the size of merchant vessels from 1970 to 2040 A.D. It anticipates no great change in cargo ships: 21,000 to 24,500 tons. However, tankers are expected to go up from a plump 250,000 to a fat 500,000 tons and bulk carriers from 80,000 to 115,000.

When one considers that tankers of the order of those now being constructed can be accommodated in only a few of the world's ports, their restricted utility in war becomes even more obvious. Presumably, in even a limited war against any enemy who can deploy major sea and air power against us, we will—unless we are ourselves physically invaded—have to move troops overseas and supply them there. Will airlift be available? If not, do we seriously think that we can, under modern conditions, move and support troops in a foreign theater with oversize vessels of the sort we have just been discussing? Cargo submarines with a Liberty ship's capacity, or even fast, relatively small, surface vessels would be infinitely less vulnerable and infinitely more practical in war. The argument that we cannot afford to subsidize them is a specious one. If we could subsidize Nasser to broadcast anti-American propaganda through the Near East, if we can endow half-savage governments whose mobs burn down our embassies, if we can give away billions of dollars worth of arms to people who detest us and who use them against our closest allies, we should be able to subsidize an American merchant marine on which we can depend in time of war—a merchant marine under the United States flag. The emphasis in such a fleet should be on nuclear propulsion, regardless of its initial cost—for that cost would be recovered swiftly, and more than recovered, in any sea war of importance. There should also be a similar emphasis in the design of new combat vessels, for thus we could acquire a fleet completely independent of an extremely vulnerable fuel supply and would deprive enemy submarines and aviation of some of their most profitable targets. In the preparatory phase, the optimum response is one which will result in maximum $M\rightarrow$ and minimum $V\rightarrow$ through the succeeding phases of expression, and no sub-optimum response can be justified by its relative inexpensiveness if it fails to produce a comparable result.

The Optimum Response: Counter-Insurgency Action

The majority of important counter-insurgency actions in recent years have been against Communist-inspired, -directed, and -assisted "insurrections." To measure their success or lack of it, it is not enough simply to state whether or not the insurrection has been suppressed, for insurrections of this sort have two aims. The first is, if possible, to overthrow the established government of the country, as Castro was able to do in Cuba. The second is, with a minimum expenditure of force, to make any pro-Western government and its allies deploy far greater forces; in short, at minimum expense, to force a vast expenditure of money and men, time and treasure. Some Communist-led insurrections have succeeded in their primary aim. More have failed. A few have been suppressed completely. But generally their second aim has been achieved. From any cost-efficiency standpoint, they have succeeded.

The principles on which they have operated have been simple: cheapness, simplicity, obscurity, fluidity. They have usually operated against forces which, because of their more or less "regular" nature are far more expensive, much more complex, more unavoidably out in the open, more static. This comparison has held true in virtually every phase of the expression of force. By and large, our response has been first to employ ordinary weapons and techniques, and secondly to copy and perhaps even improve upon techniques used successfully by the enemy. It has not been an optimum response, because it ignores the basic difference between the forces and their aims.

Guerrilla forces, as I have pointed out, have some of the characteristics of primitive animals without highly centralized nervous, digestive, or circulatory systems, and some of the characteristics of the social insects—and they can be quite as difficult to kill. Anti-guerrilla forces, again, generally resemble more highly organized creatures: strike at any of the systems mentioned and the result can be a disabling, even if not mortal, wound. A rifle, however accurate, would be of little use against an adequately large jellyfish, nor a load of buckshot against a colony of army ants. Part of the optimum response must be to find a tool to fit the task, and a tool inexpensive enough to make opposing it unprofitable.

We have one great advantage over most Communist-led insurgents—our great scientific and technological superiority in fields where they must depend on allies far away. It would seem obvious that chemical weapons—and not necessarily inhumane ones—could be devised well suited to the conditions of jungle warfare. A free molecule knows few of the limitations of approach common to projectiles, particularly to low angle of fire projectiles, and—especially as we and our allies are certainly going to have to fight more of these wars in the future—the development of specialized weapons for the purpose would be an excellent investment. Certainly, the objection will be raised that chemical weaponry is contrary to international law, but the answer to that may lie in our refusing to accept the Communist contention that these insurrections are really *wars*. They should be considered civil disturbances—whether there is outside interference or not—and the use of chemical agents should be simply a routine police procedure in their suppression.

Another highly promising approach would be to develop electronic "bugging" techniques to the point where guerrilla movements became prohibitively hazardous and expensive. This avenue does not, as yet, seem to have been too seriously explored. Here again, a comparatively minor industrial expenditure could be expected to pay major dividends.

Finally, we should do much more to inhibit any insurrection *before* it starts. Those of our allies in less developed areas who have not already eliminated the real grievances which subversives magnify and on which insurgency can thrive, should be encouraged to follow Chiang Kai-shek's good example in Formosa and carry out necessary reforms. We should insist on this, for if we do not find the optimum response to the problem of insurgency, if we do not find a way of making insurrection at least as costly to the Communists and their followers as it is to us and our allies, we will pay a high price for our failure in the future.

National
Policy and the
Optimum Response

In a world where wars occur, there must exist a functional relationship between the several factors of the military equation and national policy. It is all very well to try to divorce the two, to say that the end-all and be-all of the military is to carry out that policy, whatever it may be—but it is also highly impractical. Regardless of other considerations, national policy must, in order to ensure anything approaching an optimum response, cut its coat according to the cloth of its military capabilities. In the short term, this means that it must operate within the framework of those military equations which immediately confront it. In the long term, it means that national policy must plan to alter the balance of these equations favorably, so that any response to situations, whether unasked-for or necessarily created, will be optimum. Sometimes circumstances will dictate that the response be immediate, sometimes that it be delayed, sometimes that there be no response at all.

The relationships are intricate, and the line between a policy limited by military considerations and one dictated by military aims can be a narrow and dangerous one. But nothing can be gained by denying or ignoring the fact that the relationships are real and inescapable. A good example of the consequences of so doing is Spain's military response in the Spanish-American War. The Spanish armed forces had been permitted to decay to an almost incredibly low level of effectiveness; in other words, Spain's long-term response had been decidedly sub-optimum. They had then, in a distinctly sub-optimum short-term response, been thrown into action against a (comparatively) invincible opponent.

Cases like this are clear. Less clear are those even more frequent instances of interminable and indecisive wars fought, sometimes out of sheer obstinacy, where military cause and effect become obscured by the announced intentions of policy and by the apologists for policy errors.

The entire question is an extremely complex, extremely vexing, and extremely *vital* one. In recent years, for instance, we have heard in the United States much criticism of an alleged increase in the influence of our professional military over matters of policy. Regardless of whether or not any of this criticism is valid, an analogous process has been going on about which there can be no doubt, and which, misunderstood, may well have given rise to some of it: the continually widening intellectual gap—referred to previously—between civilian policy makers on the one hand and the military specialists, who are supposed to execute that policy when necessary, on the other.

We badly need a new universality as a means to a new rapprochement, but if we cannot immediately have it we should at least realize the need for it, so that we may recognize any harmful consequences of its lack. Thus, respect for expertise in a highly specialized field should not be allowed to result in any undiscriminating attempt to apply its methods to a field totally unrelated, nor—as in the case of so many physical scientists after Hiroshima—in its acceptance as a magical substitute for universality. Again, the abilities needed for survival and success in one specialized area are not necessarily those demanded by another; and specialized success—however dazzling—cannot be taken uncritically as a guarantee of similar achievement in an unrelated field. Therefore, because we must distrust the specialist's claims to instant universality, and because we today need universality more than ever before, we should do everything in our power to define it and to encourage its rebirth. Granted, nowadays no man—civilian or military—can memorize and understand all stored knowledge, all "maps" of structure and process, but he can get a very fair functional picture of the totality: of how knowledge is acquired, of how it is stored, of how it is scientifically and intuitively applied. He can understand where our acquisition and application of knowledge and power is taking, and can take, the human race. It is such an understanding that we should strive for, because it is essential to any major optimum response we may attempt against the challenge of the world, not only in matters military, but in the great problems of peace as well.

The Optimum Response: A Summary

The term "optimum response" is descriptive only. It is not magical; nor is it any substitute for the intensive study and careful application of those laws which govern the two-sided expression of destructive force against vulnerable objects and objectives. The ideal response in any military situation, immediate or eventual, is the achievement of a favorable critical imbalance, and the optimum response is simply the degree to which it is physically possible either to realize that ideal or to prevent the enemy from realizing it, given the values of M$\rightarrow$ and M'$\rightarrow$, V$\rightarrow$ and V'$\rightarrow$ implicit in the situation itself. However, the fact that the optimum situational response may fall far short of the ideal should never be allowed to divert the commander or the policy maker from that ideal or its desirability.

In war, and especially in the upper magnitudes of war, there can be one criterion and one only: *maximum result from minimal investment.* However, as the phrase *minimal investment* can be appraised *only in terms of the result pro-*

186   *Decisive Warfare*

duced, we must not fall into the error of expecting miracles from inadequate force and allowing considerations of economy—rather than military relevance—to dictate our strength either quantitatively or qualitatively. Keeping in mind the ideal of the critical imbalance and decisive action —before we even judge the question of an optimum response—we should ask ourselves, *Will it work when measured by that standard?* Then, if time is available, we should be ready to discard anything that will not work when so measured, and to adopt or devise that which will. This applies to weapons, to instruments and instrumentalities, to methods and techniques, and, inevitably, to individuals.

The rule holds true for any and all the categories of war, for any and all the phases of expression of force, both in the positive and negative aspects.

Even granting, except for the extremely unlikely possibility of an absolute technological surprise, *that* a *decisive* first category war is a contradiction in terms, because of the fact that the society of nations is still an anarchy we must be as well prepared as possible to fight wars in any category. Therefore, in terms of what we know of the processes of war and of modern science, I think the following measures should be taken:

1. Elimination of concentrations of vulnerability afloat and ashore. This means the phasing out not only of giant combat ships, but of enormous merchant vessels as well. Ideally, it also means the decentralization of power and water sources and, if at all possible, the decentralization of our largest industrial and population centers.
2. An accelerated development of self-contained, probably nuclear, power plants for naval vessels of all major types, for the merchant vessels on which the armed forces must depend in war, and for armored vehicles on land. The effect on logistics and maneuver phase vulnerability would be almost unimaginable.

3. An accelerated development of submersibles both for cargo-carrying and combat purposes.
4. A reëvaluation of weapons relevance, and an extended program of special weapons design, particularly for jungle and guerrilla warfare.
5. A reëvaluation of the "tactical" role of manned aircraft with a greater emphasis on co-operation with extended-range armored forces.
6. A continuing reëvaluation of military methods and techniques, in choice of materiel, supply, training, and personnel utilization, especially of those copied or adapted from civilian counterparts. The purposes are different and the survival rules are different. The military should be governed by military *considerations*, which are imposed by the processes of war.
7. A foreign policy designed, not to Balkanize the world, but to unite it—and one based not on the fallacy that the unstable bomb of threatening war can be legislated out of existence by a tangle of disarmament treaties, but on the far more feasible idea of de-fusing that bomb by exploring hitherto untried avenues of agreement and of common interest.

We stand today at the threshold of space, the threshold of the greatest of man's adventures. If we allow the engines which can take us to the stars to destroy us, and perhaps the very earth itself, that adventure will die with us. If, on the other hand, we come to understand the inevitabilities of modern war, perhaps we can at last realize, *as a race*, what mankind has never fully realized before: that when the values of the equations of war reach a certain point, war ceases to be a means to survival—and that indeed it is necessary only because men make it so. I hope that this study of war's processes may make some contribution, however small, to that realization.

Index

189

www.ingramcontent.com/pod-product-compliance
Lightning Source LLC
Chambersburg PA
CBHW031509270326
41930CB00006B/319